Ironing It Out

Seven Simple Steps to Resolving Conflict

Charles P. Lickson

Crisp Publications, Inc.

Ironing It Out
Seven Simple Steps to Resolving Conflict

by Charles P. Lickson

Cataloging-in-Publication Data

Lickson, Charles P.
  Ironing It Out: Seven Simple Steps to Resolving Conflict
  ISBN No. 0-56052-379-4
  1. Conflict 2. Conflict Resolution 3. Psychology
  Library of Congress Catalog Card Number

Fourth Printing

First Crisp Publications Edition Revised

Printed on Recycled Paper

Contents

· ·

Contents (continued)

Preface

· ·

This is the second edition of this book. Since writing the first edition in 1991 and 1992 I have learned much about conflict—in all of its glory. I have learned by engaging in professional mediation practice, by teaching and training mediators and by my own experience of conflict in the intervening years. As I said in the preface to the first edition, conflict often manifests itself as something bad. It often doesn't feel good. In the years since writing the first edition, I have participated first hand with people in conflict—as I mediated their disputes, as I counseled them in how to handle their situation and as I coached them and their organizations in how to deal with it. One of my goals in writing this book was, at the time of the first edition, and still is, to make people in conflict understand themselves and others better and to begin to feel good again.

On a personal note, I want to extend a special thanks to Mike Crisp and Phil Gerould of Crisp Publications who saw something interesting and important in this little book and decided to give it wide distribution. And a special acknowledgment is in order to those wonderful women in my life: my wonderful and wondrous wife, Bryane; my daughters Laura Stock and Karen Goneau who have both blessed me with so much including an introduction to grandfatherhood; my mother, Maxine who has always been there—conflict or not; and my mother-in-law Gertrude Miller whose support is never ending. My father, Len Lickson has been my favorite role model. My brother Jeff and sister-in-law Nancy are always my closest allies and coaches. I have had conflicts with each—and we prove over and over again that conflict can be engaged in in a loving way.

And to all others who have—and will—grace me with "good" and "bad" conflict, I salute you. Without you the book never would have been written in the first place and this edition would not have happened.

Charles P. Lickson
Front Royal, VA July, 1995

one

· ·

The Place
of
Conflict

> ❝To err is human
> To forgive is divine
> To be in conflict is the pits.❞
> —Anonymous

1

• •

Getting Started

If John Donne had been wrong when he wrote, "No man is an island unto himself," life would be simple—although quite boring. But, as we all know, Donne was right and since neither man (nor woman) is an island, conflict is inevitable.

Most people see conflict as a negative, disempowering event—part of the curse of being human.

There is another way of looking at conflict—a way in which conflict can be viewed as a potentially creative process.

The premise of this book can be simply stated: Since conflict is inevitable, why not make the best of it?

This book does not merely describe conflict or the means for resolution. It has been written for people who are in conflict or who anticipate such an event in the near future. It is not a textbook, although some descriptive background on the dynamics of conflict is included.

This book is about a process, a process which works. In fact, parts of the book have been used successfully as resource material for my seminars in conflict and dispute resolution, which have been presented coast-to-coast. The process has also become part of the conflict-handling coaching which mediators in my mediation firm are taught to provide to disputants.

This is a small book. You will not be overwhelmed by facts or statistics. Neither is it a "psychological," "legal" nor "sociological" treatise on the subject. It is, rather, a "guide-book" for navigating the rough waters around conflict situations. A major piece of the book is the recipe for the Ironing It Out process.

This work is called a "guidebook" because it is designed to be a quick, easy-reading tool—available at a moment's notice to offer some insight into dealing with the challenge of dispute.

Readers are advised to remember that dealing with conflict (as with many other issues in life) requires three distinct steps:

1. Recognizing the situation at hand.

2. Assessing the nature of the conflict.

3. Taking action to resolve it.

We have all experienced conflict and thus, we may feel as if we can recognize it easily. But conflict comes in many shapes and wears many guises. To assist in the recognition and assessment process, the book looks next at "why conflict?"

The purpose of Section One is to orient you to the ground of being of the book—the essentials of conflict.

In Section Two, you will learn the Seven Simple Steps for ironing out conflict and see how each step fits into the intricate puzzle of conflict resolution.

Observing the seven-step process work in real-life cases is the subject of Section Three. This section is designed to provide you with insights into specific situations. How someone else applies the process can serve as a powerful aid to your application of the Ironing It Out steps to your own situations and relationships.

Finally, in Section Four, I offer some material designed to assist and support you in applying the process in your life. I also include certain sources where help is available from outsiders if you should feel that is necessary.

As you journey along this book's path, you will see through the Conflict Case Studies how different people deal with their tough issues of conflict. You will also be asked to engage in some introspective thinking about yourself and conflict and you will be asked to be open to the possibilities of being coached in how to deal with conflict.

All of the material in this book is designed to assist you in learning how to turn the "curse of conflict" into a "course *in* conflict" with immediate, identifiable results.

Conflict is popular these days. In fact, I have even heard the expression that "conflict is a growth industry." Conflict is big business. Much has been written, video- and audio-taped, taught, coached, whispered and even shouted about conflict—especially in the tough, high-tension times in which we live. Authors, seminar leaders and other "gurus" of academe, "well-being," business and industry have discovered the fertile field of conflict as a gold mine.

My hope and expectation is that you will find this little book to be different from what you may have already seen, heard and read—and you will find it the same. It will be the same in that it acknowledges the awesome power of conflict over human beings. In fact, I refer often to the fine works of other authors, commentators and teachers who have preceded me. This book will be different in that it will explore new ground, reveal simple truths and provide a realistic, workable process for changing the course of conflict.

Conflict wears many hats and rears its head in many different situations. In organizing my thoughts for this book, I decided to utilize several basic situations to help readers connect with the subject. The principles enumerated in the book and the process work equally well for a conflict between parent and child, business associates, labor and management and governments and their constituents.

Conflict can be both generic and specific. While there may be some specific hints along the way in how to deal with specific situations, most of the material applies to all kinds of conflicts.

I think you will find the exercises, case studies, charts and forms to be powerful mechanisms for learning. If you can add a case study from your own or an associate's experience, you could well add to a breakthrough for someone else. It is my expectation that this book may open a two way communication between me and you. Please feel free to communicate with me at P.O. Box 607, Front Royal, VA 22630 or through the publisher.

This book is one you just might want to keep handy. As with all recipes, you may commit the basics of the Ironing It Out process to memory. When it is time for the perfect meal (i.e., in times of real need), even the best of chefs go back to the cookbook. You, too, should feel free to come back to this book for refreshment, recollection, encouragement and support.

Read on, savor, reflect and enjoy questioning conflict.

2

●●●

So Why Conflict?

"The most constructive way of resolving conflicts is to avoid them." So stated the late Justice Felix Frankfurter of the U.S. Supreme Court in the case referred to by lawyers as the *Western Pacific* case.[1] But, as we all know, life doesn't always seem to work out that way.

It would be nice if we could all heed Justice Frankfurter's advice and avoid conflicts altogether. But, let's face it, anytime two people occupy the same space, conflict is inevitable. Get any two people together and they will find a way to disagree about something. So conflict is here and here to stay. And, if we can't avoid it, we must learn to handle it. But for some reason most methods for handling conflict are unknown or unused.

Why bother dealing with the conflicts that arise in our daily lives at home, at work and at play?

Aside from the fact that conflict isn't much fun for most people, health practitioners these days will point to the harmful consequences of stress. And most stress, I think we can agree, is caused by conflict of some type.

Thus, whether you are reading this book because of conflict at home, in business, at school or anyplace else, you have acknowledged the role conflict plays in your life and have decided to learn more about it. Even more importantly, you have decided to learn how to deal with it in a positive way.

This section of *Ironing It Out* is an introduction to recognizing conflict when it is at hand or about to happen. It also deals briefly with the special dynamics and personal upsets represented by individual and group conflicts.

This book will walk you quickly through conflict, assist you in recognizing the type of conflict you are experiencing and give you practical guidance in resolving the underlying situation causing the problem. It will also provide you with some valuable resources where you can find outside support and conflict resolution assistance.

As with each section of this book, you will find in Section One text material plus a number of case studies where you can learn by comparison to real-life situations, tests you can give yourself or another which can help give you insight on where you stand on certain points, checklists to guide you through the process and to use as tools for future conflict situations, and exercises to assist in absorbing the new skills offered by the Ironing It Out process. All of these are designed to maximize both your enjoyment and use of this book.

A SIMPLE DEFINITION OF CONFLICT

Conflict is that feeling or condition which occurs whenever you face an unpleasant situation created by you or someone else. The condition of conflict differs from "just feeling upset" in that conflict always presents at least two possibilities or choices, one or both of which may be agreeable or not agreeable.

Conflict can show up in almost any circumstance of our lives and has been with us practically since we were born. A few generalizations about conflict can be stated up front:

- Conflict can be internal (felt only by us about an issue in our own mind).

- Conflict can be external (felt by us and at least one other person).

- Conflict can be direct (aimed at you).

- Conflict can be indirect (not aimed at you personally).

- Conflict can be individual (personal or shared by two people).

- Conflict can be shared (by three or more people).

Whichever kind of conflict we are talking about, it usually appears to the person or persons "in conflict" in two ways:

1. Something perceived as unpleasant and which causes one anger, upset, guilt or pain.

2. Something one does, thinks or says which causes him/her to be upset because of mixed feelings about it and the choices one feels he/she may have to make.

So, either kind of conflict can be engaged in directly (something done or said to you) or indirectly (something done or said around you which affects you and causes you upset).

An argument between you and your business partner is an example of a direct conflict. An indirect conflict, on the other hand, might take the form of a disagreement with a company policy—even though the policy was written for all employees. The policy was not aimed at you personally, but it affects you.

Conflict can also appear as an emotion. You probably have found yourself torn between two or more choices and suffered what may be called "internal" conflict.

Thus, conflict can manifest itself externally, where there is some type of dispute with another person or persons, or internally, where the dispute is inside.

Conflict can also hide behind other masks. As you will see later, removing masks is essential to conflict resolution.

At this point in the book, it is sufficient if you can see the following general points about conflict:

- It can be active or passive—you either create it or you feel it when it is created elsewhere.

- It can be direct—done to you.

- It can be indirect—not done to you, but you feel it.

- It can be external—expressed in your reaction to outside circumstances.

- It can be positive or negative.

- It can be internal—a reaction to difficult choices which have to be made.

- It manifests itself in many ways and many places and often wears the guise of anger, stress, upset, sadness and even illness.

As we progress, you will begin to see and learn how to discern certain types of conflict.

Among the essentials of conflict which you will learn as you study this process are:

- How to characterize conflict and notice what issues the other person or persons have "at stake."

- How to recognize the masks we wear and why they often stand in the way of ironing out conflicts.

- How to use the Ironing It Out steps and what they can mean to you, not only in the resolution of conflict, but also in the preservation of relationships.

3

. . . .

Getting Down to Basics

The generalizations about conflict having been stated in the prior chapter, it is now time to relate you to this book on a very personal level.

I have done this by creating certain ground rules or presumptions necessary for you to understand (and agree to) as you go on in the book and the Ironing It Out process. I call them: The Basics.

Some of the following basics may seem obvious, but they are an integral part of your basic training in the process.

These presumptions are designed to give you a framework within which to understand what I say. If you look carefully, you will also note they contain valuable information about how we see conflict.

Remember, it is only after we are able to objectively observe how we see conflict that possibilities for dealing with it constructively can occur.

THE BASICS

1. *Human beings see things often not as things are, but as who they are.* Your own rose-colored glasses are fine.

2. *Nothing is obvious.* I shall not assume you already know a point I intend to make.

3. *Simplicity doesn't mean unimportance.* Thus, if I make a suggestion which seems simple, it should not be misinterpreted as unimportant. Life can be simple or complicated. We choose the path. For this book, I have chosen "simple," although we certainly will deal with "complicated" issues.

4. *Conflict is a normal part of life.* If there is no conflict in your life perhaps you should check your pulse.

5. *Dealing with conflict involves two responses.* Human responses are either (a) automatic (uncontrolled) or (b) learned (controlled).

6. *The automatic response to conflict may or may not be alterable.* You will see that it is up to you—or it isn't!

7. *The learned response to conflict can impact our whole life.* The result can be very positive from both a physical and mental standpoint.

8. *Humans have certain "styles" of behavior.* These styles dictate in great measure the automatic response to conflict.

9. *Humans want (and need) to communicate with each other.* This is true despite the fact that it doesn't always look that way.

Much of the remainder of this book will show you how understanding these ground rules/presumptions will empower you to "iron out" conflicts (often before they occur). I intend this process to be "light." That is, I expect to offer you a chuckle here and there while this "simple" process unfolds. You may even be moved. I hope you always will be touched.

One final note, as with all processes involving behavior modification (which is a fancy way of saying changing the way we do something), the participant must be willing to play. This willingness is vital to the process. I can only presume from your continuing to read on that you *are* willing to play.

In spite of the fact that conflict is deeply and automatically ingrained into the reality of who we are as humans, learning to deal with it need not be difficult or hard to put into practice, although altering some automatic responses to conflict may not feel good on occasion.

"Ironing It Out" is, in fact, a simple process and one which in many ways seems obvious. I would consider my job as author (and your drill sergeant in conflict-resolution basic training) well done if, after reading this book and doing some of the exercises, you were to say: "I didn't learn anything new," but also felt compelled to add "However, I never saw it quite that way before."

It has been said before: "There is nothing I can teach you that you don't already know. All my teachings are but reminders that your innermost knowing will confirm"— Yogi Amrit Desai.

So, let's begin this simple process by reviewing in a little more detail each of the underlying ground rules/presumptions mentioned earlier. We will then look back at conflict, this time with a view to seeing how we each play the conflict game and how resolution can be achieved.

MORE ABOUT THE BASICS

1. *Human beings see things often not as things are, but as who they are.*

I think we would all admit that even objective criteria can be altered by our own subjective view. If we are having a bad day, the ride to work seems longer, the traffic worse and the car performance less than good. If we are having a good day, everything looks wonderful. Being aware of this human tendency toward subjective evaluation or judgment is essential to remember as we get further into the Ironing It Out process.

2. *Nothing is obvious.*

While there are certain physical truths to the world (the sun rises and sets, water seeks the lowest level, what goes up must come down), for purposes of this book and the process described, nothing about the nonphysical world will be assumed by me as obvious to you, the reader.

In many years of law practice, mediating and teaching, I have learned to assume nothing. Thus, if I seem to state the obvious please bear with me. I have found from leading seminars and teaching college courses that it is always necessary to start a discussion from a common base point. If the common base point is too common for you, have patience, I'll move along quickly.

3. *Simplicity doesn't mean unimportance.*

One of the ironies of life is that it is both simple (we breathe simply and naturally, often without even noticing it) and complex (emotions such as love can wreak havoc on our being) at the same time. The Ironing It Out process operates in this fundamental paradox. You will see that the process is simple. The steps are easy. Execution of these easy steps can be awfully difficult at times, however, and takes a degree of persistence as well as commitment.

In this book and process, each step is important—whether you judge it as simple or complex. Keep in mind Ground Rule No. 1 above: you see the world through your eyes. What may appear simple to you may be overwhelmingly complex to someone else.

If it appears simple, relax and enjoy a simple lesson for a change.

4. *Conflict is a normal part of life.*

This does not make it right, correct or justified. It just is that way. Humans can't help it, we are conditioned to conflict at an early age. The first time we were hungry and cried for food as an infant and didn't get our way, we were in conflict.

When, several years later, we wanted to stay up late at night and our parents said "go to bed," we were in conflict. When we fought with our brother or sister or friend over toys or when we wanted a certain book read to us and they wanted another, conflict reared its ugly head.

In fact, conflict appeared so early in each of our lives, it wasn't even recognized as such and was just accepted as something that was there. It might have been unpleasant or even fun, but it was and always will be a part of the human condition.

What to do with it and about it becomes the challenge and, in great measure, is the goal of this book and the Ironing It Out process.

If I were to promise you that after reading this book, there would be no conflict in your life, not only would I be deceiving you, I also would be offering to remove one of the most natural and potentially rewarding mechanisms we have for breakthrough and accomplishment.

So, I do not offer to remove conflict from you or you from it. Instead, I offer an opportunity to master conflict— to harvest it for your own and others' benefit.

5. *Dealing with conflict involves two responses: (a) automatic, or (b) learned.*

Psychologists, anthropologists, educators and others will say that by a very early age (perhaps as early as seven years), we have learned most of what we'll ever learn in life. This early learning manifests itself in the automatic response mechanism to most situations we face including conflict. If our early response was anger, fear, rejection—it will continue to be the "automatic" response to conflict throughout our life unless and until another way of response can be learned.

Your automatic response to conflict is part of who you are and contributes to your individual, distinct personality. I would not presume that I could take this away, nor would you want me to.

In this book, I will offer you a method for learning a new way to deal with conflict. This way will be designed to offer you a choice when conflict arises. Remember, this book does not provide an instant lobotomy. You will still be you for better or worse—in all your glory and splendor. You will also have a choice in how to deal with conflict: via your automatic reaction or by your new learned, empowering process.

One important note applies throughout the book but is extremely relevant regarding your learning to have a choice in the area of conflict: you have to be willing to learn and you have to be willing to see the potential power in something other than your "automatic" reaction. If you are willing to do both, you will enjoy the rest of this book and the process it teaches.

6. *The automatic response to conflict may or may not be alterable.*

Now, you are saying to yourself, Lickson is a typical lawyer. He hedges his bets wherever possible—even when writing. The truth is that some people will not be willing and thus able to alter their response to conflict. In dealing with conflict (which means dealing with people), you must be prepared to confront the person who is truly stuck in his/her automatic response and is unwilling to even listen to all the wonderful empowering magic you will be able to dispense after reading this book. Do not despair. Even for these stubborn souls, conflict can be given a new look.

Suppose you see yourself in the category of having an unalterable automatic response. The first question to ask is: why did I buy this book? Next, you might ask yourself who runs your life: (a) you or (b) your thoughts, judgments, concepts and automatic responses.

If you are who I think you are, the answer is: "you" run your life *and* you have automatic responses.

Great, now are you willing to assert your command over yourself? If so, the following affirmation might help:

"I am in command of myself. I recognize that I have thoughts, judgments and automatic responses. Sometimes these are for my higher good. Sometimes they are not. However, down deep it is I who run the show, not my thoughts, judgments and responses."

If you can say the affirmation to yourself (preferably out loud looking directly at yourself in a mirror) and get a feeling that you mean it, great. Read on, have fun and finish the book and learn the Ironing It Out process.

If you cannot say the affirmation or accept its thought with sincere meaning (other than feeling foolish at being discovered by someone else talking to yourself in the mirror), perhaps it is time to pass this book on to a friend.

So, are you willing to play or not?

7. The learned response to conflict can impact our whole life.

Your willingness to play in this wondrous game of life and to be open to a new way of dealing with conflict is bound to alter your way of seeing many things. You are about to give yourself a gift—an insight into the nature of humanness which can change your outlook forever.

If that sounds a little scary, that's fine. There is no hocus-pocus. In fact, as I said earlier, I promise I will not reveal to you anything you didn't already know. But, I will also promise you I will present those old facts in a fresh and revealing perspective, which *will* alter how you deal with conflict in your life and can also alter your outlook on life in a positive, healthy way.

Conflict and its cousin, stress, put people into hospitals, mental institutions and graves every day. Armed with the insights from this book and the Ironing It Out process you will have a choice not only as to conflict, but as to your health.

8. *Humans have certain "styles of behavior" which dictate in great measure their automatic response to conflict.*

Most observers of humanity, including virtually all professionals in human resources, now accept that each person has a personal style. Tessa Albert Warschaw refers to it as ". . . what fascinates" or what is memorable about a person. As she says in her book *Winning by Negotiation,*[2] style is ". . . what is left when you walk out of the room. It's the expression of your essence, as individual as your signature or thumbprint."

Style dictates how a person reacts to virtually every situation in his/her life. In actuality, style refers to the manifestation of the reaction, not necessarily the reaction itself. This stylistic manifestation of reaction (part of the automatic response referred to above) is so important to the subject of dealing with conflict that it deserves discussion here and will appear again throughout the book and process. In the next chapter we characterize conflict in terms of people's reactions to their "interests" in the outcome. As you will see, how each of us plays out our "interests" is dictated, in great measure, by our "style." Dealing with conflict is, after all, dealing with people.

Resolving conflict is therefore, resolving people issues. To be better able to do that, we must look deeper into how people act in general and their automatic response around tough issues (i.e., their style).

Various authors, lecturers and practitioners in the human and healing arts have categorized style. The Stuart Atkins "LIFO" Training refers to four "Orientations to Life."[3] This human resources development tool breaks style or orientation into those people who are:

1. supporting/giving (cooperative, dedicated),

2. conserving/holding (systematic, analytical),

3. controlling/taking (persistent, urgent), and

4. adapting/dealing (tactful, flexible).

In the LIFO look at humans, people are categorized by their goal orientation. Thus, supporting/giving people are seen as trying to be helpful to prove their worth. The conserving/holding people like to go slow and be sure of what they do. Controlling/taking types are competent and seek results. Adapting/dealing people appear to the LIFO process as trying to be popular to fit into the group.

Certain style descriptions and methods for testing become fashionable as others go out, but one thing remains: all people have a way of manifesting their reactions to circumstances in their life. The observers of these manifestations or styles generally fall into two categories themselves. They either see distinct style patterns which cause a person to fall plainly within one style type or another or they see fewer distinctions and more areas of stylistic overlapping.

However styles are categorized, several general types do appear. Based upon my own observations over many years of dealing with people in difficult situations and my research to prepare this book and my conflict resolution training programs, I would divide people as follows:

- those who love a fight (for the sake of the fight itself, not necessarily the need to win)—"the Fighters."

- those who have an uncontrolled need to be right about everything—"the Perfectionists."

- those who will compromise to make things less tense—"the Pacifiers."

- those who never take positions on anything—"the Neutrals."

- those who see life as an opportunity to live which requires openness—"the Realists."

Dr. Warschaw details characteristics and traits of her style choices together with a primer on how each style should respond in a negotiation with another style.[4] While I agree that understanding the other person's style (as well as your own) can be a powerful element in resolving conflict, I do not see it as essential. Instead, I would suggest that a person's style gives the observer an extra tool in dealing with the situation at hand. This tool involves the psychology of relating to people of different types.

There is a danger to be considered here. All too often writers and teachers "over-psychologize." That is, they look to psychology to provide quick fixes or tricks for dealing with people. I do not mean to minimize "style chemistry" in conflicts between human beings. Rather, the Ironing It Out process will concentrate on methodology for resolving disputes based on the situation using processes (to be described later) which apply equally to individuals of all styles.

I agree that when there is a breakdown in the resolution process, studying the dynamic of individual human-chemical-emotional reactions (i.e., personality and style) takes on greater importance. For example, the person you are in conflict with could have the kind of style which manifests itself in total stonewalling. Reaching him/her with a view toward resolution will be impossible without knowing how to deal with his/her style.

For purposes of going forward from here, it would be helpful if you think about the style description on the chart which follows and pick out which of the styles best describes you. I fall into the category of observers who see much overlapping in styles. Thus, I don't offer any of these categories as absolutes. For example, you could easily be part-fighter and part-pacifier and that will be fine for our purposes.

Description	Short Name	Typical Reaction to Conflict
1. People who love a fight for the sake of the fight.	*Fighters*	They will go to the wall, raise hell, be flamboyant, threaten violence (but hardly ever do it—since they are often cowards). Their "positions" may not be correct, but they will present them loudly and forcefully. They will often win by their bullying tactics, but aren't bad losers because they already got their jollies in the contest.
2. Those who need to be right about everything.	*Perfectionists*	They will only hear their own side (position) and need to be convinced that the other side is right (a virtually impossible task) before they will change. And if they lose or compromise, they will bear a grudge because they knew they were right anyway.
3. Those who will compromise to make things less tense or even look good.	*Pacifiers*	They will pretend everything is O.K. They will bend over backwards to make things nice, even if it means not truly resolving an issue. They are dangerous because they never reveal where they really stand.
4. Those who never take positions on anything.	*Neutrals*	They will not assert any positions and will avoid confrontations even more so than the Pacifiers. They too are dangerous because they will take an internal position, but never express it, so completion is impossible with Neutrals.
5. Those who see life as an opportunity to live fully.	*Realists*	They view breakdown as opportunity. They will be strong about their view, but will also be open to hear the other side and look for breakthrough where possible. Realists know that relationships and positions are separable and will deal with conflict with a view toward separating the relationship from the conflicting positions.

9. *Humans want (and need) to communicate with each other . . . and they want to resolve their conflicts.*

When John Donne differentiated man from an island, he reflected not only his poetic talent, but also his many years of experience and observation as a cleric. Thousands of volumes have been written about man's place with respect to one's fellow man. From the Bible to the Social Contract to the New Age Movement, it has become an axiom of humanity that individuals need each other.

L. Ron Hubbard, the controversial founder of Scientology and author of *Dianetics*[5], discovered that his original formula for survival of man could not work without relationship to others. The Four Dynamics of Dianetics connect humans not only as individuals but also as a group with a view to the survival of all humankind.

This need for mutual association and cooperation has also been called "Natural Compassion." In a wonderful book on service to others, Ram Dass and Paul Gorman refer to Natural Compassion as an automatic response in most people to needs of others. To these authors caring for another is seen as an essential part of the "quality of being" for people.[6] In fact, their perception is that the impulse to care (and communicate) with another is instinctive. To Dass and Gorman, this helping communication generates inside us feelings of well-being because it satisfies a natural urge.

Dr. Brent Hafen and Kathryn Fransden summed it up well in their book *People Need People,*[7] where they looked at the vital link between relationships and health.

Following the San Francisco area earthquake of 1989, *Newsweek* magazine did a cover story on how people help each other in emergencies and disasters. The authors looked at various theories on why people help each other, but could not reach a conclusion as to motivation. The article only noted that it seems automatic for people to help each other in group crisis situations.

I could list a myriad of other comments and observations on the need of humans to communicate with each other. And, while I stated earlier that nothing in this book will be considered obvious, I will amend that statement here somewhat by calling upon you to accept the premise that communication is essential to human activity. And, as we will see, with communication, resolution is not far behind.

COMMUNICATION—THE ESSENTIAL TOOL IN THE PROCESS

We will see in the next section of the book exactly how important communication is to the process. In fact, I can flatly state that no conflict can be resolved without using the communication mechanism. For the record, that does not mean that the communication must be received (although that is clearly preferable) but *it must be sent!*

Just as conflict is part of our daily lives (whether we like it or not), so is communication. In the most isolated monastery in Tibet, communication takes place every day. While it may not look or sound like communication in our high-tech frenetic understanding of the term, it is still communication of the basic needs and wants of the community.

As you read on, please remember: communication is an essential step in the process.

Remember also these background basics are designed to assist the process in working for you.

Having looked at the basics of conflict, it is time now to look at how conflicts reflect what is *at stake* for the parties.

4

• •

What's "At Stake"?

In order to consider your role and the role of the other party in the issue which confronts you and appears as conflict, it is necessary to reflect upon the issues in the minds of both of you. These are sometimes referred to as "wants," but, in fact, as we shall see shortly, there is a distinct difference between "wants" and "needs."

It is unlikely the dispute can be resolved without addressing the "needs" of the parties. It is these "needs" which will determine the "bottom line" in any negotiation. "Wants" can be called "icing on the cake"—i.e., nice to get, but not essential to satisfy the minimum interests necessary to resolve a conflict. "Needs" in a negotiation can reasonably translate to "interests" and "interests" determine what is "at stake" for parties in the issue.

The interests of the parties usually can be best addressed by looking at their particular approaches to the dispute. This is sometimes referred to colloquially as "where they are coming from."

To determine "where a person is coming from" in a dispute, it is necessary to know something about the nature of the dispute.

We have already seen from our general conflict discussion that any time two or more goals or positions compete—conflict follows. Further, almost any situation which causes discomfort in a person can be called conflict.

It is helpful here to say a quick word about the dynamics of "internal" versus "external" conflict.

This book offers a process for dealing with certain types of conflict—those which result in disputes. These special conflicts are those which arise from external sources and where *Ironing It Out* can help.

What we address here are conflicts where there exists a dispute between two or more people which can be resolved. Internal conflicts do not present that type of opportunity.

That is not to say that internal conflicts are not valid or important to one's decision making. Internal conflicts are basic to our value systems and often function as the judge in right/wrong decisions. These conflicts are also important to basic ethics and morality. If people did not feel conflict over certain conduct, they would never ponder questions of morality. Tied very closely to this is the issue of conscience.

Internal realizations are not internal conflicts. If this sounds a bit obtuse, perhaps an example from my own experience will help:

Some years ago when I was working as an in-house corporate lawyer for a medium-sized corporation, my boss, the general counsel, asked me to deliver a group of securities from midtown New York to the broker in the Wall Street area. It turns out these securities were bearer bonds with a value of approximately $400,000. I realized as I packed these documents into my attache case that I could head toward Wall Street and just keep going until I got to Brazil.

I also knew that I would never do that. Thus, my knowledge of what I *could do* was a realization only. If I had contemplated *actually doing it* but found myself perplexed internally over whether or not it was legal or moral, that would have been an internal conflict.

As I reflect on examples of internal conflict in my life, I recall many situations where I found myself confused as to what action to take. An internal conflict occurred when I decided to leave the greater New York-Connecticut area and migrate to Virginia. Not only did I wonder how well a Connecticut Yankee would do in Queen Charlotte's Court (I lived for several years in Charlottesville which was named after Queen Charlotte), but I also was torn about leaving my daughters, parents, friends, relatives and roots. On the one hand, my wife and I wanted to leave and on the other I was reluctant to leave so large a part of my life.

I faced an internal conflict because two choices competed for my decision. While the decision I made was not easy, I resolved my conflict with my declaration that I did the right thing for me at this stage of my life. I would be less than honest if I denied occasional feelings of wonder at the decision, but I no longer have internal conflicts about my move. There are, in fact, other emotions—loneliness for family and friends or guilt, for example.

While this book is not designed to offer solutions to internal conflict, such conflicts are very real and qualify as "conflicts" in the truest sense of the word.

In fact, certain methods described in this book might very well apply to an internal conflict. But, since one person represents both sides of that kind of conflict, the Ironing It Out process as a whole would not apply. So, in order to narrow the wide-ranging definition of conflict where this process can work and to consider what may be "at stake," let us now eliminate internal conflicts.

Of course, that still leaves us with conflicts of almost every type imaginable. So, let's try to narrow the focus even more.

CHARACTERIZING CONFLICTS

We could characterize conflicts by subject matter (and, in fact it is necessary to do this a little later when we describe specific hints for dealing with specific conflicts).

We could characterize conflicts by the people in the conflict (and, in fact, we did that when we talked about style earlier and we'll do that again when we revisit style in Section Four).

We could characterize conflicts by where they appear—e.g., the boardroom, the bedroom, the schoolroom, etc. (and we'll do that indirectly both here and later).

We could characterize conflicts by the method used to deal with them—i.e., discussion, negotiation, mediation, litigation (and we'll do that when we look at the different methods for dispute resolution later).

So, if we could characterize conflicts by each of the general categories above, which are we to use?

The answer is: none of the above and all of the above. This paradoxical answer emerges because at this stage of your study the best way to approach different types of conflict is by looking at the "interest considerations" of the parties in the conflict.

In a few pages, you will take the "At Stake Test" where you will do an exercise designed to delineate your particular interests in an issue of importance (perhaps a current conflict). To understand the interests context of conflict better, use the following tool.

Harvard's Fisher and Urey in their monumental little book *Getting to Yes*[8] analyze the differences of parties by their interests. They do this for the purpose of seeking areas of mutual interest in order to reach agreement in a negotiation context. While that is perfectly valid and very helpful, their "interest categories" provide, in my opinion, an insightful delineation of the areas of conflict.

As they point out, if one party cares more about one aspect of an issue than the other, conflict is assured. They cite the following general types of cares by each "side" to an issue:[9]

One Side:	*The Other Side:*
form	substance
economics	politics
internal	external
symbolic	practical

current .... long term

results .... relationships

hardware/things .... ideology/concepts

progress (liberal) .... tradition (conservative)

other cases .... this case

looking good .... results

personal issues .... group satisfaction

This list is by no means complete or absolute, but it points out the differences in approach which lead to conflict.

Other authors have created their own lists.

For our purposes at this stage, we will attempt to focus the conflict not by subject matter, the people involved, methods used or the forum for dispute. Instead, we will borrow from Fisher and Urey and focus on the *differences in approach* underlying the issue in dispute, i.e., the conflict.

This also presents us with our first Conflict Case Study opportunity:

Conflict Case Study No. 1

Jean was a rather conservative divorced woman who was working as an outside helper in a landscape nursery. Frank, a political liberal, was the son of European parents who had founded the nursery. He was known for his liberal views regarding women's rights, but had many hesitations about hiring Jean to do what amounted to, in Frank's view, men's work.

When Jean applied for a new, higher-paying position driving a plant delivery truck for Frank, she was turned down because, in Frank's view, even though he believed in equal opportunity for women, this was not "a woman's job." He also told Jean that the man he hired, Jim, was big and strong and had kids and needed the money. Jean was quick to point out to Frank that even though she was not the trouble-making type, he had been unfair to her. She reminded him of all the good physical work she had done for him and that, although she was not now married, she too had kids and needed the money. Most importantly, Jean assured Frank that she could do the job.

It was too late. Frank decided not to relent on his decision to hire Jim.

The situation at the nursery soon deteriorated to the point of hostility between Jean and Frank and a great strain between Jean and Jim, the new driver. Conflicts appeared on almost every issue among these three people and it was soon clear that something had to be done.

Frank contemplated firing Jean although he admired her and knew her to be an excellent worker.

For her part, Jean contemplated seeing a lawyer and filing a sex discrimination charge against Frank.

Now ripe for adversarial action, this conflict required professional intervention. Jean probably had a valid claim against Frank and hesitated to file it only because her conservatism kept her out of court. Frank might have gotten away with firing Jean, but he admired her emancipated woman's approach and she did her job well.

Jean soon reached the point where her anger and upset were affecting her work. She asked for a meeting with Frank's dad, who had founded the firm and who had become friendly with Jean during his occasional visits. Frank's dad suggested the three sit down together to see about resolving the conflict.

A resolution was reached by promoting Jean to foreman of a work crew at the same money she would have received driving the truck. Jean was happy and made some excellent suggestions to Frank about how he could improve crew dispatching, which saved Frank money. The conflict had given the parties a creative opportunity to look for a solution. In this case, the result was a win for all concerned.

Now, let's analyze the root of Frank and Jean's conflict in terms of the interests of the parties as outlined above.

The underlying political/philosophical differences (Jean's conservatism, Frank's liberalism) were not an issue, although clearly Jean's conservatism restrained her from taking legal action and Frank's liberalism allowed Frank to both understand and admire Jean.

The conflict arose out of a misperception by Frank of Jean's family situation and capability. Frank had considered form ("women's work") and not substance (Jean's true ability to do the job). Jean was motivated by economics (she needed the higher paying position) while Frank's internal conflict was between an economic motive (getting more work out of a man) and a political one (his pro-women's rights thinking).

Frank's hiring decision was made with a view toward the short-term or immediate capability of Jim and not with a long-term view of Jean's output over a period of time. He also believed that other cases and not this one were the place for a pro-woman's rights stand.

If you looked at the case of Frank and Jean further, you could very well find applicability of other interest positions from the list above. It is clear that this dispute arose out of "interest conflicts" between the parties. It was both an external conflict between Frank and Jean and an internal one in that each had conflicting feelings about what to do (as is true in most conflict situations).

A resolution of Frank and Jean's problem could only come from dealing *with the interests of the other* in attempting to reach a solution which satisfies *the minimum number of interests necessary* to create a change in the other's viewpoint.

When you look at conflict in terms of interest considerations, you must always be mindful of the interest considerations of both sides. While knowing these may not always lead you to a solution, not considering the interests of both parties is certain to keep the conflict going.

Later in the book you will find some specific hints at dealing with interest considerations during the resolution process.

In thinking about characterizing conflict, I gave great thought to general categories of subject matter. I probably could have filled several pages with material about legal conflicts, personal conflicts, family conflicts and business conflicts. In truth, as we have seen, conflict implies competition for action. This competition is affected by many things including the subject matter, but the bottom line is the *interests at stake*.

It is time to look at the first practical exercise in the book. This is a simple-sounding test which can be surprisingly revealing in its outcome. When confronting an issue of particular importance or a conflict which carries a special "charge," consider taking this test *before* you do or say anything else.

THE "AT STAKE" TEST

1. Ask yourself what the other side has at stake here.

2. Ask yourself what you have at stake here.

3. Ask if these "at stake" issues are totally incompatible.

4. If they are not incompatible, look for mutuality of interest.

5. If they are incompatible, look for a basis for resolution not inconsistent with either your or the other side's "at stake" issues.

6. If you cannot come up with any possibilities for either 4 or 5 above, seek the advice of a third party to assist you with answers to this test regarding the conflict.

7. If, after talking with a third party, the two of you cannot come up with any possibilities for 4 or 5 above, it is time to seek professional conflict resolution assistance. (A listing of some sources is located in Section Four of this book.)

This "At Stake" Test can save you hours of heartache and be a powerful little tool in your quest to resolve conflict with a minimum amount of trauma. It can also become the framework of the Ironing It Out process detailed in Section Two of the book.

A handy form (The Conflict Issue Checklist/Questionnaire) to accompany this test and identify the issues in conflict is located in Chapter 19.

Most of our discussion has centered on what may be characterized as "individual conflict." But, what happens when a group conflict is at hand? Rather than indulge in a wide-ranging discussion of group conflict, suffice it to say that it pulses with its own special characteristics. These include the emergence of what I call an "un-leader" who seems to want to control the group action. Un-leaders are usually driven by their own personal agenda which may have very little to do with what is really "at stake" for the rest of the group.

Group conflict is unique in some ways. It differs from individual conflict primarily in the lack of control any one person has over the dynamic and in the feelings of the group feeding upon themselves. Thus, the first challenge in looking at group conflict is to see if a mechanism can be devised for assessing the "at stake" interests of the greatest number of participants and then trying to find common ground between those interests and the interests of the rest of the group.

As we think of group conflict, and group dynamic, we think of psychology. Let's now take a closer look at conflict and psychology.

CONFLICT AND PSYCHOLOGY

As tempting as it might be, I should not leave a discussion about the kinds of conflict without at least a comment on psychology's view of conflict. To a psychologist, conflict is viewed as a special kind of drawing or tearing of the mind in several directions. The textbooks put it this way: "When an individual must make a decision between incompatible or contradictory needs, desires, motives, wishes or external demands, he or she experiences conflict."[10]

Traditional views of psychology speak of the mental manifestations of conflict and break it into four general types:

1. Approach–Approach Conflicts

These are the good news conflicts. They involve choices which have to be made from two or more positive or "desirable" alternatives. These are usually the easiest to resolve. The classic example is the child in a toy store who is told to pick out one toy.

2. Avoidance–Avoidance Conflicts

These are the bad news conflicts. These are the ones where the person is stuck "between a rock and a hard place." In these conflicts, both choices are unpleasant. These are most difficult to resolve because either choice is undesirable or unworkable for some reason. These conflicts are among the leading creators of stress. An example of this kind of stress would be a soldier's decision to shoot someone. If he shoots, he could violate a moral principle against killing. If he doesn't he may be killed.

3. Approach–Avoidance Conflict

These are the conflicts that look like good news, but are really bad news. These too are difficult because there is both attraction and repulsion involved. An example for me would be to climb the Eiffel Tower in Paris. I would love to see the City of Lights from up there, but my fear of heights would probably win out. One could characterize my feelings about making the tower climb as *ambivalent,* in that I have both positive and negative feelings. Often the response to these conflicts is to do nothing.

4. Double Approach–Avoidance Conflicts

These are good news and bad news conflicts. In these conflicts, the choices have both negative and positive pulls to them. An example would be: You are

accepted at two colleges. One has an excellent reputation and good social life but is very expensive; the
other is inexpensive but is not so great academically
and has virtually no social life. Resolution is not
easy in these conflicts because there is a tendency
to waver between the choices. These are the most
common conflicts we see around us.

To the psychologist, conflict is seen in association with
its near neighbors: frustration and stress. Also to be considered in the psychological approach are the major behav-
ioral reactions and internal survival mechanisms the
psyche uses to deal with or avoid the situation at hand.

We can see a variety of reactions depending on the
circumstances of the stimulation event (sometimes known
as a "stressor").

Reactions to frustrations which may arise out of a conflict situation where progress toward a goal is impeded
include the following:

Persistence—keeping at it.

Increased response—trying even harder.

Circumvention—getting around it.

Aggression—breaking through with force.

Blaming—looking for fault or a scapegoat.

Escape—avoiding the issue.

Withdrawal—avoiding everything.

The short descriptions above certainly are not comprehensive, but they should give you a sense of the reactions
which you can identify in yourself.

The anxiety reactions which one feels usually find
expression in *defense mechanisms*. These fall into the
following general categories:

Denial—refusing to accept because of the pain involved.

Compensation—distracting oneself from the main
   issue by some other event or achievement.

Fantasy—looking to the unreal for escape.

Isolation—separating thoughts from each other to avoid internal conflict.

Projection—putting one's feelings or reactions onto another person.

Rationalization—justifying thoughts or actions by creating "reasons" for them.

Repression—unconsciously shielding oneself from pain.

Sublimation—working off frustration by doing something else.

Regression—falling back into earlier, more youthful reactions.

While neither of the lists above is comprehensive and certainly the definitions I've used would probably make a psychologist wince in pain, they reflect reactions to the stress and anxiety of conflict. As such, they are extremely helpful. I want to clearly state that while the Ironing It Out process is not based on psychological warfare of one person against another, it is based on the principle that knowing what makes both of you tick can help.

Keeping the list of reactions in mind as you confront conflict in another will allow you the advantage of understanding what may be going on inside the other person's mind.

As I have said before, a key element in resolving conflict is communication. The ability to communicate in a context of understanding "where that person is" (mentally speaking) at the moment is very important to the chances that the communication will be effectively sent and received.

The relationship between psychology and conflict is descriptive (diagnostic) in that it allows us to perceive in some measure what is going on. It is also empowering (prescriptive) in that it can assist us in knowing what action to take in view of the mindset of the other party at the time.

So, while I want to take great care in not over-psychologizing the Ironing It Out process, I do not want to minimize the significance of the human psyche's role in the conflict resolution process.

A Practical Exercise

I recommend that you take a piece of paper and list each of the reaction/defense mechanism items listed earlier and do the following:

1. Write your own definition based upon either your own knowledge or the ideas stimulated by my few words of definition for each.

2. Look at a current or recently completed conflict situation and list how you experienced each of the items relative to the event.

3. Once you have completed the list of your reactions under 2, list what you suspect were the other person's reactions.

Save this list and do the exercise each time you feel yourself in conflict or have just finished with one. I promise powerful insights into the nature of conflict.

If one looks at the roots of conflict, one will be able to see that the internal and external challenges to our psyche arising from conflict situations have been with us for virtually all of our lives and may very well have been a part of why we are who we are today.

Developmental psychologist Erik Erikson postulated some years ago that there were eight major stages of a person's life. In each stage, beginning at infancy, a major problem or conflict arises. It is in the way this problem/conflict is handled that the person passes from stage to stage. With each conflict/challenge the individual gains strength to go on to the next stage and next challenge. Thus, to the Erikson school of thought, conflict presents an essential element in human development.[11]

This crucial relationship between psychology and conflict will be seen in many ways as we continue through our review of conflict and the Ironing It Out process.

5

• •

Assessing Your Conflict

You have now graduated from Basic Training in the Conflict Consciousness Academy. You are now ready to begin to see a new dimension for conflict—a dimension of positive possibility. The goal for the rest of the book is to move you into new thinking about conflict and to start giving you some tools for transformation of your personal relationship with conflict.

Much was said about conflict in the first part of this book. You got basic guidelines, checklists, exercises and the "At Stake" Test. All of this material was designed to orient your thinking for the balance of the book and process. Much of the remainder of the book will be practical in nature. There will still be textual material, but it will be tied into a case study, practical exercise or test.

The real work and power of the Ironing It Out process lies in *using what you learn.* Now, if you are ready for some work, some fun and some insight, read on!

HOW TO ASSESS THE CONFLICT AT HAND

On a practical level, all the knowledge and newfound conflict resolution skills a person has are worthless if they cannot be brought to bear on a real situation.

In order to bring all your powerful forces to bear, you must have a sense of the situation at hand. Thus, the assessment process is the next logical step in your study.

Assessment in the context of conflict means a combination of observation and evaluation. It is not observation alone because you are not really capable of objective observation if you are involved in the conflict. If you are involved in the issue in any way other than as a disinterested observer, objective evaluation will be impossible. Observation alone has value only for historical purposes. An evaluative factor must also be included for the assessment process to have value.

Further, we already know that we see things as who we are (Ground Rule/Presumption No. 1) and not necessarily as they are. This must always be remembered and cause us to be alert to the possible deflection of reality.

Shortly, we will look at the mechanism of centering to empower a clearer possibility for assessment of the issue at hand.

For any resolution to be effective, it must contain at least the following minimum attributes:

- It must relate to a real situation.

- It must be handled in a manner appropriate to the real situation.

- It must be played out fully.

Assessing the conflict may sound easy at first, but it is not quite as simple as you might think. This is because our emotions are usually tied into the conflict and our rational mind is often not allowed to be open enough to assess. Also influencing our ability to view is old baggage left over from our early home life. According to psychiatrist Dr. W. Hugh Missildine, we carry into all of our decisions, including those dealing with difficulties and self-evaluation, images of our own past childhood. We must each be aware of this and, as Dr. Missildine warns, correct this view without self-criticism, if we are to see objectively.[12]

So, the first step in the assessment process is to open the mind. I'm not talking about open-brain surgery either. By "opening the mind," I mean allowing the issues at hand and other "stuff" which may be going on in your mind or occupying your thoughts to go away.

You may ask: how do I do this? The single word that best answers this question is a word which has become very popular lately—"centering."

Centering

The process of centering, which is introduced here in the context of assessing the conflict, will be of value to most of the work of the Ironing It Out process.

Centering is coming to a place where you are clear of other issues. In essence, you travel to the center of your personal universe. The object of centering is to become rooted in your mind/body. Only from such a place is a person capable of clear thought.

Many people spend long hours, even days or years trying to become centered. Others are able to do it through a brief, quiet internalizing process. Still others are not ever able to become centered. Most people don't even know what it is.

I found it necessary before I went into a courtroom or a heavy negotiation to take a moment to gather thoughts, clear my mind, visualize the place I was about to enter in a most positive way and breathe life-giving clear air into my mind. My favorite spot to do this was in front of the windows on the second floor of the Superior Courthouse in Stamford, Connecticut, where I did much of my court work.

Whenever I would go to a new courthouse or other facility, I would always look for a little corner somewhere (usually in a hall, sometimes a lawyer's lounge and sometimes a library) where I could do a little centering process.

Doing the process did not take very long and, as far as I could tell, I never made a fool of myself doing it. In fact, until I put these words in writing, most people probably never even knew I did any process—including me. That is, I never knew that what I was doing was centering. I thought of it as "psyching myself up," getting ready or some other process. The term "centering" wasn't popular then.

And, even if the term had been popular, I probably wouldn't have called what I did "centering." I used to be rather stiff and conservative in those bygone lawyering days and I would have thought of centering as a process for Hare-krishnas or bohemians. So, if I did it, I certainly wouldn't have admitted it to anybody then.

I readily admit to centering now. In fact, I always advise people to do some type of centering or internal reflection or mind-clearing process before looking at or dealing with a difficult situation. Before starting one of my private mediation sessions I center myself and invite the parties to consider doing it in whatever way makes them comfortable.

This centering activity can be a confrontation for some people. I remember training a respected commercial trial attorney at a big-city law firm. He could not bring himself to engage in such an activity as centering and he did not know how to advise others to do so.

Let me make it easy for you. It may simply involve being quiet for a time. In the following section, I share with you a relatively simple process.

A Centering Process

One process for centering which I learned several years ago and have always remembered is the following:

- Close your eyes and take a relaxing breath.

- Think of a restful place—it might be a shady wooded spot or an open meadow, it might be a resting spot by a bubbling stream, or it might be a warm beach by a crystal clear sea.

- With your eyes closed, go there in your mind. That is, visualize yourself there—enjoying the peace and comfort of that special place.

- Visualize the people involved in the issue or dispute at hand. Try only to see their physical characteristics without having your judgments come up at this time.

- Visualize the issue or problem in your mind and try to see the problem as an object of some kind separate from the people.

Perhaps the problem can be placed in the form of a box or some other tangible object. If you cannot transform the problem into an object, that is fine. Try to resist the temptation to lump the problem and the people into one.

- See yourself observing the people and the problem independently from each other.

- Say to yourself in your mind in that special place: "I observe now without judgment."

- Open your eyes and see your surroundings. Try to retain the image of the people and the problem.

Having gone through the centering steps, you are now in a better state mentally to think about and evaluate the situation.

At this point, you may be saying to yourself: This is ridiculous. I won't have the time to go through this whole, long process—especially if there is an immediate situation at hand which requires some quick evaluation.

That is a reasonable thought to have because it would seem as if the centering process described above is time consuming and requires peaceful concentration in a quiet place. Well, it does not have to be long in time and certainly does not need a quiet place to work.

Crowded courtroom halls are not the quietest places in the world and I still found a way to quickly do this process. In point of fact, it may very well have taken longer to read about this process than it would take for you to do it. To prove how easy it is to do, try this powerful little practical exercise. You will need another person to assist you or you could use a tape recorder.

A Practical Exercise

1. If you have an assistant, find a comfortable position. You may sit, stand or even lie down.

2. Decide what problem, issue or conflict you are going to look at in this exercise.

3. Close your eyes and take a deep breath.

4. As you let your breath out, try to release all other thoughts and issues.

5. Have your friend read slowly each statement from the centering process above and pause for a moment or two between statements while your mind responds to the suggestion. Notice how quickly the "stuff" comes into your mind.

6. After you are told to open your eyes, think about what happened to you and, if you can share with your assistant, tell him or her what happened.

If you don't have an assistant or prefer to do this exercise by yourself, that is fine. Record on tape the statements referred to above and play them back while your eyes are closed. It may be a good idea for you to find a blank tape to use and keep for this and other processes you may want to have near you (in the car, at work, at school, etc.).

You may be surprised at what comes up for you in doing this exercise. Can you see the power in closed-eye work? If you cannot that's fine. There will be many other opportunities to learn process techniques while eyes are open.

Now that you understand centering, you are able to move on to the next stage of assessing the conflict situation.

THE *STOP, LOOK* AND *LISTEN* FACTORS

Assessment of anything requires perception. In this book on solving problems, the prolific psychologist and teacher Michael J. Mahoney refers to essential steps required before solutions to problems can become possible. These are the situation, the perception, assumptions, feelings and action necessary to be taken. As he says: "Our reactions to life events depend in part on how we view them."[13]

In our discussion, we move now to how we view events with some coaching on possible alterations in the way we see, hear and assess what is happening. The alterations suggested are designed to set the stage for dealing effectively with the conflict problem at hand.

The three little words "Stop, Look and Listen" are three of the most powerful words in the conflict resolution process. They could be applied to virtually every step of the process, but are paramount to assessing the conflict situation at hand, which is why they are introduced in this chapter.

Stop—reminds you that before going any further in the process, discussion, argument, fighting, suing, or anything, you need to evaluate. In order to do this, you must take pains to stop all other outside distractions to be able to look and listen (as described below). This does not mean that if your children are playing outside, you should not listen for them or that if a pot is on the stove you should ignore it. It does not mean that if you are at the office, you should not answer the phone if it rings.

"Stop" does mean that you should be prepared to let the process of looking and listening take place in as mentally clear a space as possible. It requires you to ask yourself questions like the following:

- What am I dealing with?

- Is it a dispute at all?

- Is it a position or opinion by the other side?

- Are they serious?

- Is there room for discussion or play?

- What do they expect from me?

- What is the bottom line apt to be?

- What happens next?

Evaluation implies far more than mere observation as suggested as part of the centering step. That is why Dr. Mahoney refers to "perceptions and assumptions" about the situation. He even advises listing the "problem" according to various categories including "perception" and "assumption."[14]

Evaluation requires interpretation of the situation by comparison to known criteria. These criteria may already be known to you (through your own knowledge of the subject or by your past experience) or they may be available to you through another source. Outside sources for comparison include other people, known standards in the field or subject, ethical or moral principles or coaching sources, such as seminars, books, tapes and the like.

Look—reminds you that to evaluate you must see what is going on. This does not mean seeing only what is presented or offered for your view, but seeing everything you can.

Looking at someone, a situation or thing sounds easy. You probably know that many of us live our lives hiding behind a mask or playing a role. Masks hide persons and issues from view and inhibit fair and open assessment in two ways: (1) They are difficult to see through (that is, the person you are trying to see can hide), and (2) they often obscure the vision of the observer (that is, your own mask can deeply affect how well you see out). We'll go into how and why people wear masks in the next chapter.

You may also recall Ground Rule/Presumption No. 1 (we see the world as we are, not as the world is). This natural subjectivity poses a challenge to looking at any situation.

To effectively assess the conflict situation at hand, you must be able to find a way of truly seeing it and not your interpretation of it.

How, you could well ask, do I know that what I am see-ing is what is really there and not my interpretation of it?

If you seek support of another in confirming your view, you will quickly learn whether or not your observation was accurate.

Sometimes it may not be appropriate or possible for you to ask for assistance of another. In such a case, try asking yourself the following questions:

1. What am I seeing?

2. Is it really that or is my mind adding its own interpretation?

3. If I were writing a news report of the person, situation or event I am seeing, how would I describe it?

Listen—to both the sound of the situation (that is what is being said and other audible parts of the issue) and what your internal mind is saying to you about it.

The word "listen" in this context refers not only to the physical act of allowing sounds in, but also to the mind's voice telling you what is happening. This "mind voice" has been variously called "inner self," "inner child," "spirit guide" and various other names. New Age writers are hav-ing a field day with names and descriptions of this "mind voice." There is even a strong spiritual movement in this country and elsewhere which believes this inner voice to be a manifestation of God or the Holy Spirit.

In truth, you listen to your intuition. Shakti Gawain, author of the popular *Creative Visualization* and *Living in the Light*,[15] has become one of the gurus of intuition. A foundation premise which can be seen in all of her writ-ing, including *Return to the Garden*,[16] is: trust your intu-ition. Gawain is convinced and convincing in her asser-tion that intuition can guide a person to effective change, better health, more money and good relationships. She refers to intuition as "that knowingness that resides in each of us."[17]

Even if you don't accept the proposition that your intuition reflects a higher power than you, I'm sure you will agree that you have an intuition and that it has a valuable service to perform. In fact, you can be certain that intuition will tell you something about the situation you are assessing if you will listen to it.

Listening also means hearing on the physical level. Just as our preconceptions and judgments affect what we seen, so too do they effect what we hear. Basic Ground Rule/Presumption No. 1 could just as easily have been worded: "We hear the world not as it is, but as we are." Another way of saying it is: we hear what we want to hear. Knowing this puts us on alert to try to be as objective in our listening as we are in our seeing.

As you travel with me through the word journey of this book, I will point out impressive sights along the way. First stop: the words "Stop, Look and Listen." They are words of power in the Ironing It Out process!

· ·

The Ironing
It Out
Process

"*An apple a day keeps the doctor away.***
*A conflict a day keeps the lawyers in pay.***"**
—Anonymous

6

· ·

The Process in a Nutshell

Now that you have a feel for the background of conflict in your life and the lives of people around you, you are ready to learn about a very practical, step-by-step method for resolving conflict using seven simple steps.

These steps, which I call the *Ironing It Out* process, will provide you with a chance to pool all your knowledge about conflict and put it together into a meaningful process.

If we were to consider the introductory material your basic training in conflict and resolution, the process steps would be advanced training.

In my seminars and consulting, many people get nervous about the field training portion of their learning effort. They think they will be required to practice weird experiments on the children, the neighbors or the mother-in-law.

There is no need for nervousness, since you will always be in command.

As you read on and work on some of the exercises in this section of the book, you will never carry out an order that you don't issue to yourself (although I may make a suggestion or two).

You may find yourself using these steps in happenings in your life other than conflict. That's O.K. The publisher does not make an extra charge for these successes. They should be thought of as fringe benefits available only to Honor Graduates of the Ironing It Out Academy.

The steps are listed below. They will be discussed in some detail as you read on. If you can master the power of the Process, it could have an important effect on your life.

As you read these steps, notice that your eyes appear to be looking at a staircase or at the side of a pyramid. Remember, as you travel *down* these steps, you will, in actuality, be traveling *up* a path toward greater personal effectiveness, less stress, better health and more fulfilling relationships.

Be prepared to engrain these Seven Simple Steps into your mind and your heart. They belong in both places:

> **Step 1:**   **Remove All Masks!**
>
> **Step 2:**   **Identify the *Real* Problem!**
>
> **Step 3:**   **Give Up a "Must Win" Attitude!**
>
> **Step 4:**   **Develop Several Possible Solutions!**
>
> **Step 5:**   **Evaluate Options and Select a Solution!**
>
> **Step 6:**   **Communicate in a Manner Certain to be Received!**
>
> **Step 7:**   **Acknowledge and Preserve the Value in the Relationship!**

We will now look at each step in more detail and the role that each step plays in the total Ironing It Out process.

7

STEP 1:

Remove All Masks!

As we have seen from earlier discussion, no conflict can be resolved unless people and not their pretenses show up. Sincerity is the ideal mindset for conflict resolution.

It may be that sincerity is difficult, if not impossible, because of the particular situation in which you find yourself. Sincerity is not easy to muster when one is in either an offensive or defensive posture (as most of us are when we find ourselves in stressful circumstances).

If we cannot achieve sincerity, at least we must aim for authenticity. Being authentic means not hiding behind masks. It means showing up as yourself.

Sometimes we don't even know who we are at the moment of conflict. In some cases we may have been living an inauthentic life for a considerable period of time because of other things going on in our lives, including roles we play at work or in our relationships. In these cases, finding the "authentic you" may not be very easy. It can even require outside help in the form of friendly conversation, loving advice or professional intervention.

To be able to maximize the potential of this process and especially this step, you must be prepared to do whatever it takes, including getting outside help if necessary to be present in the process as yourself.

Each step in the Ironing It Out process is a critical part of the delicate balance of the whole; therefore, as part of your learning this section of the book, you will be asked to do a short exercise featuring each step. At the end of this chapter, you will be offered suggestions on practical exercises to use and perfect the Ironing It Out process on your own.

Because of the way the steps reflect the accumulated knowledge you have gained from earlier reading in the book, commentaries on some of the steps are longer than others. An exercise follows each step.

Some of the exercises involve little stories with questions at the end. Others involve self-reflection processes. As with every exercise in the book, writing down your answers is best, but answers can be dictated into your tape recorder or done in your mind if that is easier.

> Step One in the Ironing It Out process is:
>
> **"Remove All Masks!"**

STEP 1 EXERCISE
("MIGHTIER THAN THE MASK")

1. Think of a role you have played in your life or a mask you have worn.

2. Think of a conflict you have been involved in or the conflict facing you now.

3. Think of (or write down) the way your role or mask would play out the conflict.

4. Think of (or write down) how the real you would play it out.

5. Think about which of these two aspects (your mask or you) has the better chance at resolving the conflict.

You are now ready to go on to Step Two.

8

• •

STEP 2:

Identify the *Real* Problem!

A conflict shows up in many ways. It manifests itself in many incarnations. You must somehow look through all the garbage to find out what is really at issue to be able to resolve the problem. Thus, at Step Two in the process, you are asked to identify the *real* problem.

As with many of the steps in this chapter, you might think: "That's easy for you to say, but how do you do it?"

As we proceed further, I shall offer several suggestions on how to add these steps to your everyday decision-making processes and especially how to use them at time of crisis.

Several examples follow of how what appears to be "at issue" is not the *real* problem:

- You may think that you and your spouse are having a conflict over how late your child should be allowed to stay out at night. When you look behind this *apparent* problem, you may find the *real* problem is your conflict with your child as to who will be the boss.

- You may think that your boss and you are at conflict over whether or not you need to travel to see a customer in person, as you suggest, rather than handle it by phone, as your boss suggests. When you look behind it, you may find that the real problem has to do with what you are being paid and you believe it is not enough. You may think that business trips with some good meals, comfortable hotels and nice rental cars are owed to you because you are being underpaid.

• You may think that you and your spouse are in conflict over jobs around the house. The real problem, you might discover when you look deeply, is your frustration at not being engaged in full-time, salaried employment.

In each of these scenarios, the *real* problem lurked somewhere underneath the *apparent* problem. Resolution of conflict cannot be achieved until the process can address the true problem.

Sometimes finding the true problem takes some real effort. If a resolution is really what you want, it is well worth the peeling away of the onion skin layers to find the problem underneath the problem.

As we have seen, people are often unable or unwilling to acknowledge what is really the problem. The "At Stake" Test (in Chapter 4) will help get at the truth of the conflict.

The following short exercise should also help.

This exercise is an eyes-closed exercise. Someone should read the following directions to you or you can tape them and play them back so you can do this exercise with your eyes closed.

STEP 2 EXERCISE
("PEELING THE ONION")

1. Visualize a problem you are having.

2. Pretend that problem is a large onion. Try to actually see the problem as a huge onion in your mind.

3. Now, peel away a layer of the problem/onion skin and see what problem or issue lies underneath.

4. Take a moment to be with that new problem, then peel away another layer of the problem/onion skin and see what lies there.

5. Notice the new problem you see which lived underneath the layer of problem/onion skin you just peeled away.

6. Now try to peel away another layer and continue to do that until you have no more layers to peel or you see no new problem.

7. It is likely the problem at the bottom (or under the skin of the other problems) is the *real* problem.

8. Open your eyes and proceed, if you wish, to resolve the real problem using the balance of the process.

The ability (even called by some an "art") to peel away the surface issues to get at the *real* problem is a prerequisite for good problem solving and an essential step in the Ironing It Out process. How can a problem be resolved if the reality of it is not apparent to you?

If you are still stuck with this one, please reread Chapter 5 where the *Stop, Look* and *Listen* tools are discussed in assessing conflict.

9

●●

STEP 3:

Give Up a "Must Win" Attitude!

"Must win" attitudes belong to players who never ever really win at life. They may sound like winners and even occasionally look like winners, but in fact, these players compete so hard all the time that a good part of life passes them by.

When things get tough and problems and conflicts arise, the "must win" players become the "position" players. They are the ones who will go to the wall to defend a position and will go down screaming and often take as many people as possible with them when they go.

Resolving conflicts from "must win" positions is virtually impossible, unless you are dealing with Neutrals on the other side (see chart in Chapter 3).

If you are dealing with Neutrals, the conflict will never truly be resolved because by their nature, Neutrals harbor resentment and never forget their victimization at the hands of the "winner." Be alert, because Neutrals are the type who often try to get even someday.

Note: No conflict can ever be considered resolved if a party wants to get even someday.

The Fighters from our chart also take positions. They too "must win," although they will give in.

"Winning" a conflict is an oxymoron like "cruel kindness." Conflicts are not won! They are RESOLVED.

The following exercise illustrates the shallowness of such a Pyrrhic victory. The exercise involves a story followed by some questions.

STEP 3 EXERCISE
(WINNING THE "EMPTY" VICTORY)

STORY: *Harry Rosen practiced law. He was good in court. He was what is called a "winner." He worked for a firm which represented insurance companies in defense of claims against professionals for alleged malpractice. His primary clients were doctors and hospitals. It was in a particular case against a hospital that Harry found himself in court opposite a lawyer representing a client who had clearly been mistreated by the client hospital. The insurance company had already settled the case brought by the plaintiff against two physicians for improperly using an experimental medical process upon her in surgery. Another lawyer had handled the case against the physicians. but would not handle the case against the hospital.*

Harry felt he could beat the new lawyer in the case against the hospital. He was certain the lawyer could not find an expert witness to testify that the hospital did not have a review committee as required by law when experimental procedures were to be used. The fact that the hospital did not have such a committee and that Harry knew they were in violation of FDA regulations did not matter. Harry's firm had to settle with the other lawyer in the case against the physicians. They would not even talk about a settlement with the new lawyer.

They now decided it was time to win and so the firm sent Harry into court. Harry's position was that the plaintiff could not prove her case. It did not matter to Harry whether or not there had been a violation or that the woman suffered injury because the hospital had not properly warned her of the results of this experimental surgery. What mattered was winning and standing on the position of "lack of proof" which Harry believed should be enough.

After three weeks of trial before a judge whom Harry knew used to represent insurance companies, the plaintiff rested. Harry had been surprised when experts were marched into court to prove the allegations against the hospital. Harry felt as if the case could be trouble if it ever got to the jury; however, when the plaintiff's lawyer asked if a settlement were possible before the defense (the hospital) presented its case, Harry remained firm. He soon moved for a directed verdict and to his surprise, the judge granted the motion. The plaintiff was out of court and Harry had won again. Harry had taken a tough position, had never wavered from it and it paid off.

About a year later, the same attorney approached Harry and his firm with a different case against a different hospital. The issue was informed consent about an operation. The plaintiff was a 70-year-old man and the operation was a vasectomy. The hospital claimed it didn't need to have particular consent to this operation because the man was scheduled to have a prostate operation which, in the hospital's view, included a vasectomy; besides, the man was 70 years old, so what did it matter? When the new plaintiff's attorney approached Harry to discuss a peaceful resolution, Harry, the winner, stood on his "plaintiff can't prove it" position again.

After several years of delay and great heartache for the plaintiff including the loss of his wife, the case came to trial. Harry had beaten this lawyer before in a case against a hospital and felt the jury would laugh at this man's claim. Harry stood on the "plaintiff can't prove it" position even though he knew the hospital had performed the vasectomy without specific consent in violation of not only general standards, but also the hospital's own rules.

After almost a month of trial, the jury went out. Harry still did not budge and refused to offer any settlement. The plaintiff offered to take $50,000 to settle. Harry said "not one penny!" The jury awarded the plaintiff $180,000 damages.

Even then, Harry, the winner, did not give up. He appealed the verdict and more than a year later and after thousands of dollars of additional fees and expenses from the hospital and insurance company to Harry's firm, the state supreme court upheld the award. Harry's client now had to pay the original judgment plus interest and statutory fees.

QUESTIONS: Think about these and be honest in your answers to yourself or in discussion with another:

1. Did Harry win the first case?

2. Did Harry win the second case?

3. Was Harry's position a service to himself or his client?

4. Could Harry have changed his position in either case and what difference would it have made in the result?

5. If you had been the attorney for the hospital, given the limited facts at your disposal, how would you have handled the first and second cases?

Can you see that having taken a "must win" position, Harry not only eliminated any possibility of resolution of the problem, but also did his client a disservice? Even in the first case, where Harry won the court case, do you think his conscience or moral judgment might question how well he truly did?

In fact Harry was not a winner. He was a loser. Any time a dispute is handled from a "must win" approach, loss of some kind is inevitable. What may look like a win on the surface is often either a loss or results in being stuck in the "status quo." The issue must be RESOLVED rather than won.

Even lawyers are learning that. It has taken many years; but alternatives to traditional dispute resolution are growing rapidly, even in the legal profession.

How can you tell the difference between "resolving" something and "winning"?

"Resolving" involves a permanent disposition of the matter. It means that while people may not be happy about the result, they all agree it is over. "Winning," on the other hand, is more temporary and can leave a very negative aftertaste.

Often the so-called "winner" is not happy with the result. He or she may think he/she is happy with the "win," but usually the "result" is not enough. In addition, the relationship is often preserved by "resolving" and often destroyed by "winning."

10

· ·

STEP 4:

Develop Several Possible Solutions!

If life were certain and the results pre-ordained in some way, then there would be only one solution to each and every conflict. But, reality is not like that and most situations could go in a variety of directions. It is up to the players to determine from any number of possibilities how the conflict will play out.

Ignoring the problem, giving in to the other side or resisting him or her "tooth and nail" each eliminates possibilities for peaceful resolution. The Ironing It Out process requires development of several resolution choices, for good reason.

There is a school of thought which is quite popular these days which says that you should pick a target or objective, focus on it and go all out to get it. This philosophy often views development of choices or fall-back positions as detracting from the determination to obtain a result.

While this kind of determination and commitment are required for some things in life and are certainly helpful to the decision to resolve conflict, the specific elements available for a resolution must come from choices. The alternative to developing choices is an "all or nothing" mindset. All-or-nothing players end up with "nothing" far more often than they end up with "all."

Emphasis in this step of the process is on agreeing that choices of potential solutions are desirable. Developing choices and evaluating them for a particular situation are part of the next step. The exercise which follows Step 5 applies to both Step 4 and to Step 5.

11

. . . .

STEP 5:

Evaluate Options and Select a Solution!

If we can agree that all-or-nothing attitudes invite confrontation and are blocks to conflict resolution, it is clear that another approach—one which looks at choices or options—is necessary.

From choices which are developed as possibilities for resolution can come the breakthrough needed to Iron Out the problem.

Development of the particular options which could be available to you obviously relates directly to the nature of the conflict. It will be up to you to create the choices. The material in this step can help you devise which choices might work.

What determines which of the possible solutions to a conflict is best in the circumstances?

The answer may seem simplistic: Choose the best *workable* choice from the variety of possibilities you have gathered.

Note that there are two key words in the answer: "best" and "workable." Often the best resolution for you is not truly available. It just won't work for the other side. On the other hand, often the most workable choice holds nothing in it for you. Thus, the goal is to choose that possibility which holds the most for both of you *and* is also workable. And by "workable" here I don't just mean "acceptable" to the other side. I mean far more than that.

"Workable" as used here implies the power to move the action forward. The solution must allow for movement away from the place of conflict to a place where resolution is possible.

The formulation of several possibilities as potential solutions to a conflict assists in coming up with workable solutions for the following reasons:

- Going through the process of developing more than one possible solution forces contemplation of multiple approaches and increases the chances for resolution. Don't forget the "solution" we are looking for is "resolution," not a "win" (see Step 3 above).

- Having several possible solutions gives the other side a choice of possibilities and thus mathematically increases the chances for resolution.

- Having several possibilities also increases your own chances for finding a meeting ground for resolution. Looking for several approaches forces one out of "positional" thinking which favors usually one and not several approaches. Elimination of positional thinking has been shown to automatically support possibilities of resolution.

- The very process of developing several different possible solutions forces a testing of the sincerity of the parties. In fact, it has been shown that parties who are sincere in their desire to resolve conflict *will* develop more than one possible resolution.

The next question is: how are different possible solutions developed?

To assist in answering that question, please proceed to the exercise which follows.

STEP 5 EXERCISE
(CHOICE AS A TOOL FOR PEACE)

What follows this exercise is a Problem-Solving Choice Checklist. Your exercise is to try to think of a conflict which occurred in your life. Try to remember how you resolved the conflict and the choices you may have had available. Compare your choice for what you believed in that case was the best solution to the checklist. Ask yourself if you would handle the situation differently now that you have the enlightenment of the Ironing It Out process.

It may help to write down the results of your review and comparison of choices. If you cannot think now of a problem, pick one of the scenes from this book as the problem scenario and review that person's choices against the list which follows.

In Section Four (Resources and Forms), you will find a working copy of the Problem-Solving Choice Checklist for later use as needed.

_____

_____

_____

_____

_____

_____

_____

_____

_____

_____

_____

A PROBLEM-SOLVING CHOICE CHECKLIST

Please note: This checklist has been prepared to be used in association with the "At Stake" Test (Chapter 4) and the *Stop, Look* and *Listen* process (Chapter 5). The checklist will have value as a stand-alone aid; however, you must be able to recognize problems and your own and the other side's "at stake" issues to be able to maximize the power of the list. Remember, this checklist is designed to assist you in choosing from choices you have already created. It follows one of the premises of this book: that several possible solutions must be created before conflict can be resolved:

☐ **1.** Have I developed more than one *possible* resolution to the problem?

☐ **2.** Have I developed *all* possible choices for resolution?

☐ **3.** Is there any choice which I know I cannot live with?

☐ **4.** Have I eliminated that choice from the list?

☐ **5.** Is there any choice which I know the other side cannot live with?

☐ **6.** Have I eliminated that choice from the list?

☐ **7.** Having eliminated the unacceptable choices to both me and the other side, do I still have more than one possible solution?

☐ **8.** If I have only one solution, can I develop additional possible solutions which may be acceptable?

☐ **9.** Of the remaining possible solutions, are there any which will not work (i.e., where I know there is or will be an obstacle to resolution)?

☐ **10.** Have I eliminated from the list those solutions which I know cannot work?

☐ **11.** Do I still have more than one possible solution which can work?

☐ **12.** Of the possible solutions which can work, which choice fulfills most of my personal interests or "at stake" issues?

☐ **13.** Can this solution be acceptable to the other side or need it be adjusted in some way to be acceptable?

☐ **14.** How can the choice be adjusted, if necessary, to become acceptable to the other side?

☐ **15.** If it cannot be adjusted, is there another choice which still satisfies "at stake" issues but may be more readily acceptable?

☐ **16.** Am I satisfied that I have completely reviewed all possible choices which may be workable solutions?

☐ **17.** Have I prepared alternate choices in the event my first choice or best solution does not resolve the problem?

☐ **18.** Am I now prepared to present my first choice to the other side?

☐ **19.** Have I considered that often the chances for acceptance of a proposal lie not in the proposal itself, but in how it is presented?

☐ **20.** Knowing that the presentation of the proposal is a key element in its chances for success, have I prepared my presentation in any way (e.g., with flowers, in a calligraphy note, at a special occasion, after a good meal)?

☐ **21.** Do I now feel complete with the problem solving checklist process? If not, what else need I do for the process to feel complete?

This Problem-Solving Choice Checklist is included as a study aid to Steps 4 and 5 of the Ironing It Out process. It should be apparent that it applies equally as problems and solutions are considered throughout each of the steps and in everyday living.

12

. . . .

STEP 6:

Communicate In a Manner Certain To Be Received!

Communication has been mentioned a number of times in this book. It does not take a genius to realize that the greatest idea has no value without communication of that idea to someone else.

In virtually every course and book written on the subject of human relationships, communication is treated as the ultimate tool for positive possibilities. This is no less true for the Ironing It Out process. In fact, as I have said earlier: Communication is the *essential* tool. Without the ability to effectively inform the other side of your desire and proposal to resolve conflict, there will never be an end to the struggle at hand.

All of your wonderful work in coming up with choices, in eliminating "positions," in seeing what's "at stake" for you, and in removing your own masks will all be wasted if you are not willing or able to take the results of this good work and communicate what is going on to your wife, lover, boss, child or other conflict opponent. Thus, while communication appears as Step Six in the process, it clearly ranks at the top of all steps because it is the way by which each step is conveyed to the other party.

Communication in this context means conveying a message to the other person or group through verbal, written or other means. In the case of conflict resolution and problem solving, communication surely takes place; however, it is often filled with anger, lack of clarity and an unwillingness to move from talk to action.

To effectively communicate, one must effectively listen. You cannot reach an audience you cannot perceive. Therefore, the art of active listening becomes a key element in the communication process.

In fact, as you will see in the next part, active listening is part of the function of a third-party conflict resolver. Only when someone feels in his/her heart that his/her message has been received, can he or she listen to your message. It is human nature. You just cannot listen to someone else when you sense they have not heard you.

On the other hand, when there is a feeling that you have been truly and completely heard, you have a sense of completeness which allows you to be open to hearing someone else.

Most of us "listen" by playing in our minds our interpretation of what the other person is saying (or writing).

Is this listening or is this playing our own mind game which obstructs the ability of the other side to be able to reach us? Most studies of the subject show us that very few people listen. People hear in the physical sense that sounds penetrate their ears, but they are not listening. Instead, they are interpreting, judging, preparing their own position or thinking about something else entirely.

This kind of "communication" cannot work in conflict resolution. Thus, we must first define the concept of communication, then apply it to the Ironing It Out process.

For our purposes, let us call communication that human device using words, sounds and body language which: (a) has the attention of the other person(s), (b) tells our story (whatever it may be), and (c) allows the other person to receive and interpret it.

In this simple definition lies all the power and capability needed by us to Iron Out conflict.

Using all the knowledge we now have about resolving conflict, we are ready to:

(a) First obtain the attention of the other person.

No one will ever hear if they are not attentive. So, be certain you have his or her attention before even attempting to communicate your feelings or proposals to resolve the issue. How can you check on this? Simply ask! It is perfectly proper for you (and in fact a very powerful communication device) to say at the beginning of a communication (or even during it): "Are you with me" or "Am I making myself clear to you."

(b) Tell your story.

Your feelings, your "position" or the "facts" as you see them should be conveyed to the other side in a clear, lucid and very comprehensible way. If possible, try to avoid emotion, interpretation, or judgment in telling the story. As Sergeant Joe Friday on *Dragnet* used to say: "Just the facts, Ma'am." This isn't always easy or even possible in all cases; however, the more the story relates to only exactly what is "at issue," the greater the chances of having the communication received. All the other stuff stimulates responses in the listener which can block out what you are trying to say.

(c) Make sure it has been received.

This is necessary so your request can be interpreted and acted upon. There is a difference between interpreting a communication which has been received and interpreting the attempted communication while the other party is also trying to communicate to you (or someone else).

In the latter, genuine interpretation is probably not possible because the other person probably didn't get what was said. The listener's *concurrent* interpretation very possibly got in the way of his/her hearing.

How can you tell if the communication has been received? As stated above, it is fine to ask. Often, you can tell from the reaction whether or not they got it. If it is a hot, emotional reaction, they probably didn't get it. If what happens next is not appropriate to follow your communication, they probably didn't get it. So, try again. In fact, if you want to Iron It Out, you must be prepared to keep trying to communicate until you know the other person got it.

All this communication stuff is fine for external conflicts.

What if the conflict is internal?

You may be surprised to learn that communication can help here also. This kind of communication is not necessarily designed to be received, but rather to be sent. Thus, if you are wrestling with an internal conflict, write something about it. Write a letter, enter a diary or journal page about it, talk to someone or even yourself about it. Communication in the context of internal conflict is also referred to as "completion."

You will not be able to resolve conflict until you can be complete with it. This is true of both internal and external situations.

On the following page, you will find an exercise which can help you use communication as a resolution and completion tool.

STEP 6 EXERCISE
(COMMUNICATING WITH POWER)

1. Define, in your own words, the term "communication."

2. Now, look up the word in a good dictionary.

3. Compare your definition with that of the dictionary, checking to see how each deals with reception as an element of communication.

4. Find someone to communicate with orally. See how few words you can use to get your point across.

5. In your verbal communications, ask the person to actively listen, that is, to repeat parts of your communication back to you as you talk.

6. Ask that person to say something to you. As he/she speaks, see if you can be just with what he/she is saying without interpreting or judging.

7. Prepare a written communication of some type using as few words as possible.

8. In your next argument or strong discussion, see if you can truly listen (and hear) what the other side is saying and refrain from speaking until they finish. Ask also that they do the same for you.

13

STEP 7:

Acknowledge and Preserve the Value in the Relationship!

Resolving conflict is about preserving relationships. If that were not so, then people would not try to resolve conflicts.

Disputes could remain, fester, and destroy any home or relationship. But as pointed out earlier in the book, people do want to help each other and be in relationship. This is true even when differences arise which cause conflict.

While we read about the overwhelming increase in litigation swamping our courts, there has been an even greater increase in nontraditional means for resolving disputes. This method, known as Alternative Dispute Resolution (ADR), is rapidly growing and affords disputants a non-adversarial institutional alternative to the courtroom's adversarial approach.

A major problem in the adversarial system lies in how it affects the relationship of the parties to a dispute. As I can well remember from having represented hundreds of parties in different types of litigated disputes, the relationship can rarely survive the impact of legal warfare.

As mentioned earlier, this book is about resolving conflict—not eliminating it or teaching one of the parties how to win. "Resolving conflict" by its very nature implies preservation of relationship.

Granted, a serious, deeply felt dispute will take its toll, but where there is willingness to resolve, there exists a strong chance for preserving the underlying nature of a relationship.

One of the key benefits of a gentle process for resolving disputes is that the parties involved have a greater chance of retaining a relationship than if the traumatic forces of legalistic or violent confrontation are brought to bear on it.

The Ironing It Out process requires as the final step that parties acknowledge each other and make every reasonable attempt to look at the value in their relationship and how important that may be even in the context of the conflict at hand.

Step 7 applies equally to disputes between labor and management, supplier and customer, mother and child, husband and wife.

So, resolving disputes requires affirmation on the part of all parties that there is value in each of you as an individual, that there may be merit in the position of each, that each of you has different (sometimes even the same) issues at stake and that each of you desires the same thing down deep: resolution of the dispute and preservation of something between you.

If as you look at the conflicts and disputes in your life, you do not see preserving relationship as a reasonable goal, you are not interested in RESOLVING a dispute. You may want to end it, but without consideration of relationship issues disputes will not resolve.

This step is at the end of the process, but that does not mean that acknowledgment of each other and the value in trying to work it out comes at the end. It may. It may also come at the beginning of the process. In private mediation sessions which my firm conducts, we have a period before the meeting begins where each party agrees to enter into the process acknowledging a commitment to work it out and the value to each of them of their relationship. I also suggest that parties acknowledge that there is value for them in the position or story of the other side.

Again, at the end, I suggest that each side acknowledges the other for having agreed to go through an Ironing It Out process and that each recognizes the honesty and sincerity of the other and the commitment to relationship shown by the other in being willing to go through a dispute resolution process.

A recent real-life situation illustrates Step 7 very well:

I was brought in as a consultant to an inventor whose former agent began, in the inventor's view, to work against the inventor's interest. The inventor felt that a fiduciary duty which was owed to him by his agent was being breached and that as a result, he was losing a fortune in potential royalties.

It became apparent to me early on in this case that the invention had considerable value but that the agent was a key element to future success even if there had been a problem in the past.

The issue then became how to resolve the differences between inventor and agent giving each some satisfaction while preserving sufficient relationship between the parties to produce income from the invention.

Unfortunately, there was a great deal of anger on the part of the inventor who felt the agent had made money at his expense. On the plus side, each party was willing to communicate, through me, in an attempt to work it out.

The prospects for a resolution looked bleak (and, in fact, a resolution has not yet been realized). My challenge became to show the value to both sides of a continuing relationship. In this, I was successful. So, while these two parties to the dispute have not as yet made their peace, there exists in their "relationship" possibilities for working it out in the future and even working together again.

STEP 7 EXERCISE
(CONTACT, COMMUNICATION AND COMPLETION)

The exercise for this step is very simple (and you may find it the most difficult exercise you have yet undertaken in this book):

Think of someone with whom you have an incompletion in your life. It could be a friend who has done something for which you have not forgiven him/her. It could be a parent or child who somehow offended you and you never told him/her. It could be a worker or employer who did something you did not like. It does not have to be a big item for you or it can be.

Contact that person and communicate with him/her what it is you feel should have been said back then. Make sure your communication relates to what you feel and is not judgmental or an attack on the other person. After you have completed your statement, thank him or her and acknowledge him/her for caring enough about your relationship to allow this communication to take place.

You may be amazed at the results of such a conversation.

Congratulations, you are well on your way to a breakthrough not only in conflict, but also in relationship.

Step 7 allows for completion and acknowledgment. It not only handles the past, but also is a doorway to the future. Conflicts come and go, but it is in relationship that one finds true value in life.

As we consider the potential of this simple Ironing It Out process, let us take a moment or two at this stage of the book to review where we have been and where we are going.

We have learned something about what is behind the conflict we see in our lives (Section One). This has been presented in a simple, non-academic way designed to give background information to make learning how to resolve conflict easier.

In this Section, we have taken a look at a simple seven-step method for dealing with conflict. The process refers to *Ironing It Out*. This does not mean sweeping problems under the rug or burying your own head in the sand.

Ironing It Out means just that. It means finishing it.

The process steps empower you to complete the resolution by full consideration, selection of choices from options, communication and completion.

A method for resolving conflict which leaves issues unresolved is nothing more than provision of a storage container into which future issues are placed. In this storage container, they can fester, grow and turn disastrous.

Ironing It Out has the potential to eliminate the need for that storage container. It is a present-tense process. It deals with today, not tomorrow.

If you are happier avoiding issues and confrontation (remember the Pacifiers and Neutrals from the personality styles chart in Section One), this process is probably not for you. But if you are serious about seeing conflicts in your life as opportunities, at working out fair and workable solutions and getting on with the rest of the business of your life, you will already have seen the power and potential of the process.

It works. I know. I have used it in my personal life, professional practice and teaching.

All it takes from you is a commitment to action (not reaction) in your life.

If you are willing to learn the steps, use the forms and checklists, the potential of the process will be realized.

Let's now see the process in action in some specific contexts.

Read on.

three

· ·

Making the Process Work

"Conflict can work for you.
It has made many lawyers
and psychiatrists rich."
—Anonymous

14

· ·

Family Disputes

In discussing application of the Seven Simple Steps to particular types of disputes, we'll start with one you are sure to have experienced—a family conflict.

Family conflicts (and our reactions to them) are considered by some to be the plateaus by which we measure personal growth. Thus, these conflicts can have a very positive benefit. Of course, it doesn't feel that way while we are in the midst of an unpleasant conflict with a spouse, child, sibling or relative. In fact, it is these conflicts which probably pain us the most—and it is for that very reason we can use some tools for supporting our proper handling of the situation. As you will soon see, the Seven Steps can be those tools.

For the record, I deal with disputes between husband and wife, lovers, close friends, committed partners, even roommates as "marital issues." After discussing the marital issues, we'll move onto "parent-child issues" and then look at "other family disputes" where we discuss such things as family businesses.

MARITAL ISSUES

Marriage has been called the "never-ending journey." Along the way, the going can get tough (as anyone of us who has been married or in a close marriage-like relationship well knows).

No one has to tell you that conflicts between husbands and wives (or lovers or close friends) are supercharged with emotion, which makes them among the most interesting and difficult with which to cope.

The Ironing It Out process works on the domestic front. There is no question that these disputes present the parties with some of the greatest challenges to maintaining their cool while enlisting the process to help. Everything that has been learned so far in the process will come to bear when attempting to resolve disputes of a domestic nature.

Why are marital issues so tough? As my former physician and close friend Dr. Marty Albert (also a trained mediator) says: "It's because everything that is said or done has such a charge to it in relationship. A funny look or nod of the head at the wrong moment can be as exasperating as a knock-down, drag-out frontal assault."

Are these disputes too hot to handle?

Dr. Roger Gould in his very popular book, *Transformations*,[18] probably did not over-dramatize the point: "As a couple, we play a power game with each other that may explode at any time. Behind the facade of everyday living and loving, tensions and petty disagreements is a fusillade of hate ready to burst out when the power game spins out of control and loses its balance."

Add to all this basic misunderstandings about the psychology of the sexes and distinct gender styles in communication and you have the ideal breeding ground for trouble. Works by two female professors who have studied these differences exemplify the need for special sensitivity to the generic underlying needs of each. Carol Gilligan's book about psychological theory and women, *In A Different Voice*, points to differing "voices" which interplay and converge at the time of crisis and change.

Professor Gilligan notes differences which anyone dealing with disputes between males and females must acknowledge. Her important book addresses the experience and interaction of each sex and the "dialogues to which they give rise."[19]

Communication issues between men and women are most sensitively illuminated in Deborah Tannen's best selling *You Just Don't Understand.* Professor Tannen addresses the question of whether or not men and women even communicate in the same domain. Conversational styles can dictate much of the context of the play of dialogue between men and women. According to Professor Tannen, it is time that each sex better understood the significance of these style differences. She devotes a whole chapter of her book to "Community and Contest: Styles in Conflict."[20]

While much has been written about the difference in the sexes with new insights since the relatively recent "women's movement," the two books cited above provide an interesting and enlightening look at some basic problems underlying conflict between the sexes, in general, and especially those involving marriage or committed relationships. Add to that the years of subjugation of women by men and the newfound interest in the so-called "men's movement" exemplified by such luminaries as poet Robert Bly and you have the ideal setting for conflict (if not a battle).

This disarray each of the sexes finds itself in these days does not help in resolution of male-female conflicts. Nor is this male-female pressure new. In his Introduction to *Iron John,* Bly refers to the man's "domineering mode that has led to the repression of women and their values for centuries."[21] Sometimes, this sexual anger blasts forth in a dramatic fashion such as Beverly Gaines' *Hell Is My Husband.*[22] Most often, this feeling of disorientation between the sexes is a seething presence in the male-female dynamic and must be included in any resolution formula.

In preparing this book, I reviewed many books on conflict between the sexes and I could have cited any number of excellent texts on this topic; but I found the contexts from which professors Gilligan and Tannen approached the subject to be of profound value and so should you. Professor Gilligan, whose field is education, tries to equalize the playing field for psychological study. To her, traditional studies have misunderstood women. On the other hand, Professor Tannen's background in linguistics leads her to address methods of verbalization. For serious students of resolution of conflict both books are strongly recommended reading.

Notwithstanding the communications problems with their automatic psychological and emotional overtones, these family disputes are by no means routine and even mediators require special family mediation training before taking on these types of cases. But, they are still disputes between two (or more) parties who have certain issues at stake and who find themselves at loggerheads and like all disputes there is hope for resolution.

In family-oriented matters, including disputes between parent and child and siblings, great care must be taken to see that process steps are followed carefully with a large measure of sensitivity to the nature of the relationship and emotions involved.

To prove that the process can work, let's look at a case-study and follow the resolution mechanism step-by-step.

Conflict Case Study

Bernard and Julia had been married 16 years. While their marriage was not "perfect" in harlequin romance terms, it was a good relationship and had produced two children, Jason, age 14, and Roberta, age 11.

Bernard's personal "style" was the problem for Julia. He was so goal-oriented that he was almost obsessive about getting things done—everything. For her part, Julia believed in the shotgun approach to tasks: If she started enough projects and did something on each, eventually some job would get done.

It was in the context of this stylistic difference that the conflict between these two people first arose. Julia's unfinished projects (everything from rooms where redecorating had begun but not finished after two and a half years to completing her college education now in the seventh year of sporadic course taking) were an irritant to her husband.

Bernard initially viewed Julia's "loose ends" as cute. "O.K.," he would say to himself, "she's not organized, but she is such a good person."

On the other hand, Bernard's need to move virtually every task to completion became a serious sticking point with Julia. She, too, thought Bernard's "dedication to duty" was cute, in the beginning. When his unrelenting drive to complete everything turned, in Julia's eyes, to compulsive behavior, she too felt the pain of personal conflict.

For the first five years, Julia and Bernard valiantly turned the other cheek to the irritating foibles of the other. In the sixth year of the marriage (when Jason was 4 and Roberta was 1), they decided to place an addition on their house.

Bernard's recent salary increase at work (he was a junior architect at a local firm) should have been enough to pay the additional financial burden of their house expansion, so the couple thought at the time. He was to prepare the plans, supervise the construction and serve as an apprentice carpenter to their friend, John, who would do the construction.

Before construction was scheduled to start, Bernard would sit at his drafting table for hours designing the addition until the wee hours of the morning. From Bernard, friends would hear complaints about Julia's constant changing of the needs for the addition. Julia was blamed for making finishing the plans almost impossible.

Clearly, what should have been a happy family project was turning into a potential trouble spot for the marriage.

At Bernard's insistence, Julia finally decided what use to make of the added space. Bernard finished the plans and the work was completed. Serious difficulty had been avoided at the time because Julia had "given in" to her husband's pressure.

But she was not happy. She began to carry the feeling that the new house addition was the very manifestation of conflict between Bernard and her. The addition was "his," not hers in any way. She was determined, however, not to let her resentment control her and she began to give in more and more to avoid exacerbation of growing tension between the two mates.

Bernard viewed the relationship from an entirely different perspective. To him, Julia was the epitome of the "dizzy dame." He began to refer to her projects as the "Dizzy Dame Game" and he put up with them, in his mind, because he loved her and his children and hated confrontation.

The marriage thus percolated along for a number of years with each side tolerating the other or "giving in" to avoid trouble.

A pattern had emerged: keep the marriage going even if the contentment level was less than optimum for both parties.

All of that ended in the 16th year of marriage, when Bernard, now age 41, told Julia that he could no longer tolerate a messy house, her schoolbooks all over the place, half-decorated rooms, half-painted pictures from art lessons started but never finished, the mess in the den (now Julia's "sewing room" where she started many projects but finished few) and all of the other "loose ends" in Julia's life.

Bernard told their best friend, George—a lawyer—that he could no longer bear to live with Julia while she acted this way. He also added that he still loved her very much and that there certainly was no one else in his life and that he still hoped somehow they could get back together.

Julia was torn between heartbreak and anger at her husband's realization. She felt that she had been a loyal, loving and dutiful wife, even to the extent of depriving herself. She had thought that Bernard with his love of education and accomplishment was proud and pleased that she took so many lessons and tried to improve herself. After all, she reasoned, she had quit college to support him while he finished the fifth year of architecture school. She had also raised "his children."

Besides, she felt, living with a compulsive, internalized character such as Bernard was certainly no picnic. How dare he say he could not tolerate her habits . . . and yet, she also knew she did not want to live without him.

The conflict between Bernard and Julia was never dramatic. It was not filled with those loud yelling matches so common in marriage and which sometimes carry the threat of violence. It never really flared, nor had it ever really gone away.

It became clear to the couples' friends that something was needed and George suggested the Seven Simple Steps process. He had used them effectively in his commercial law practice in coaching clients how to deal with disputes and negotiate effectively. He spoke to both Julia and Bernard, who was now living with his friend Robert.

For Bernard and Julia, the process presented both a challenge and an opportunity. They both agreed to try it before going to a divorce lawyer or counselor.

They knew that the first step required them to really show up as who they were (Remove All Masks) and this took some thought. They way they finally accomplished this first step was to literally draw pictures of themselves and the roles they played—alone and in the chemistry of each other.

After some fairly painful moments for each, they found the identity each chose to bring to the process.

Next, Julia and Bernard prepared lists of all the things which really troubled them about each other. This was part of the second step (Identifying the Real Problem). An interesting item began to appear on both of their lists although it hid behind several other purported issues: lack of communication. The real issue for each surfaced as a perceived unwillingness of the other to share the feelings of the moment. That is, to share what each really felt and not be willing to play the cover-up game. An important secondary issue was a failure of each to acknowledge the personality needs of his/her mate.

Both Bernard and Julia then agreed that neither had to "win" in this process. The very acknowledgment of that factor had a resounding effect. It showed immediately that both were committed to preserving the relationship and had begun to restore some of their old partnership as they continued the process and the search for a resolution.

The fourth step was especially challenging (Develop Several Possible Solutions), but each suggested to the other more than one thing he/she might do which could help resolve the issues between them. Step Five (Evaluate the Options and Select One) began in parallel with Step Four.

Among the suggested choices were a trial separation, each party obtaining a special area for his/her activities in the house, designated meeting times for themselves alone and with the children and with an outside counselor. Evaluating the options is not easy within the context of the emotional charge of a *marriage in trouble, but Bernard picked the separate area in the house as his choice and Julia picked communication periods plus counseling.*

Communication (Step Six) was undoubtedly the most difficult step in the process for each of them. After all, they had spent years learning the fine art of communication-avoidance. How could they start communicating now?

In fact, it was their commitment to the process which forced each of them to communicate to the other his/her choice from the options. And each one clearly received what the other was sending.

There were some raised voices and many tears, but eventually Bernard and Julia agreed that family communication was the issue to be dealt with first.

They designated a minimum of 15 minutes per day for communication between each of them and the children. Bernard's occasional business trips were no excuse for not spending the 15 minutes in direct communication with Julia, Jason and Roberta. Further, Bernard and Julia agreed that they would spend at least one hour together during each weekend day and would spend at least one full day together a month at home or away. They also agreed to see a marriage counselor suggested by George.

Finally, in a special moment which captured the built-up emotion mixed with the strong love of these two people, each acknowledged the other (Step Seven). This acknowledgment came not only with hugs, kisses and tears, but also with conversation. Bernard thanked Julia for her commitment to the process and Julia thanked Bernard.

As a footnote to this case study, Bernard and Julia did go into marital therapy and decided after six sessions that they were strong enough to deal with the issues on their own.

Dr. Roger Gould has said that marriage involves constant renegotiation. Call it the battle of the sexes, the War of the Roses or just plain marital adjustment, the relationship of two loving, committed partners is so delicate that it presents resolution of difficulties with the ultimate challenge—get the job done, but as the Hippocratic oath says: "Above all, do no harm."

The reason the Seven Simple Steps presents such a powerful tool for resolving these loving disputes is that the parties themselves orchestrate the process from start to finish. When it gets tough or too painful, they can back away.

I'm not saying that they should cop out and quit just because it is getting too uncomfortable. On the contrary, this process cannot work without the commitment to see it through. But, I am suggesting that it can be done in a gentle and patient manner.

There is no time line for these steps. The process referred to in Bernard and Julia's case study actually occurred over almost two weeks time from the initial commitment to try it to the final acknowledgment that it worked. How forcefully to carry it out and over what time frame will be dictated by the parties and the exigencies of the situation. Obviously some crises require immediate and forceful attention. Others can be worked out over days or even weeks. Organizations and institutions sometimes take months to work things out and nations can take years.

PARENT-CHILD ISSUES

Disputes involving offspring, siblings and groups of children are probably as highly charged as disputes between mates, but with a different dynamic.

Any parent who reads this book will immediately recall many agonizing moments of conflict either *with* their child or *about* their child.

With these kinds of disputes, most of the dynamics and sensitivities referred to in marital disputes would apply, plus another very special one: disparities in power (either real or perceived).

A parent who is dealing with a child must be sensitive to the feeling of powerlessness the child may feel. Ironically, this issue would also apply to disputes between adult children and older parents who themselves might feel powerless in the struggle over the problem at hand.

I will resist the temptation to discourse (even with my limited knowledge) on the particular relationship issues flowing from the different stages of childhood development; but I will say that the age (physical or mental) of both parent and child becomes a factor in these disputes.

The next case study will illustrate a classic parent-child problem and how the process aided in the resolution.

Conflict Case Study

Dr. Fred Muller was a well-known professor at a leading state university. His books on American literature were known as landmarks in the field. He spent a year in Europe as a Fulbright Exchange professor. Professor and Mrs. Muller had two children, a boy, Fred Junior, known as Ferdy, and a daughter, Lee Ann.

Lee Ann spent her junior year of high school in France with her mom and dad, while he taught at the Sorbonne in Paris. Although she had limited knowledge of the French language, Lee Ann refused to go to the American School and instead struggled her way through a local school—the first American youngster at that school. There was no doubt Lee Ann was bright, but there was doubt as to how well she applied herself in school.

The school situation was not helped by the extraordinary scholastic accomplishments of her older brother, Ferdy, who had whizzed through college, received two masters degrees and was working on his doctorate.

Both children rebelled at their father's professional insistence that they use correct grammar at all times and read only good books. This rebellion is probably what led Ferdy into the sciences rather than humanities and led Lee Ann to attend and flunk out of three colleges in three years.

Needless to say, Professor Muller and his wife were perplexed about Lee Ann. They knew she had the brains for good work, but her resistance to academic achievement was a classic slap in the face by child to parent.

As Ferdy's reputation as a public health scientist grew, Lee Ann's stubbornness about traditional education also grew. She married at the age of 20 and promptly had two children.

It was many years before this conflict over education and training was resolved. The first step was undertaken by Lee Ann, who was by then in her forties and divorced. She decided to remove her mask as "petulant child" (Step One) and face the fact that she was growing into middle age without an education. She was thus willing to see the real problem (Step Two) and noted that it had nothing to do with her parents.

Both Lee Ann and her parents decided that there need be no winner in this contest (Step Three) and Lee Ann's dad finally supported her entry into a community college program as part of an adult degree program—a choice reached after Lee Ann and her parents had developed several possible options and picked one (Steps Four and Five). Professor Muller communicated his new support for Lee Ann's work (Step Six) by financial assistance and encouraging words which, while late in coming, meant a lot to Lee Ann, who had been certain she was a disappointment to her parents (Step Seven).

While the conflict between Lee Ann and her parents appeared to be over her education, the truth is that there were many deeply rooted psychological issues driving the wedge between parents and child.

The education issue clearly masked other problems and it was not until all parties committed to a resolution process that this thorn could be removed from what was otherwise a very loving relationship.

Note also that Lee Ann was a middle-aged adult when the commitment was made by her to use the process steps to work out the problems with her parents. She realized that her parents, who were both near 80 years old, might not be around much longer and the parents realized that they had bent over backwards to reward Ferdy for his accomplishments while failing to recognize Lee Ann's intellectual capability.

As we all know from personal experience, parent-child issues have no chronological time limit. They arise when the child is an infant or they can persist for 20 or more years or even a lifetime.

The good news is that there is no statute of limitations on resolution either. Thus, Lee Ann and her parents could decide to Iron It Out even after 20 years of persistent conflict over the education issue.

In view of the special considerations of parent-child conflicts, I feel it would be helpful to share another case study illustrating a different problem and different solution.

Conflict Case Study

Everyone was shocked when Beth and her husband Robert were divorced. They seemed to their friends and family to be the proverbial "ideal" couple and to have a wonderful relationship with their children.

It all seemed to come apart when Robert was offered a new position in New York City and Beth could not bring herself to leave Dallas.

They tried counseling, family therapy and even mediation, but Robert was determined to follow this career opportunity and Beth could not face the thought of leaving her parents, friends and her Texas roots. What hurt her so much was that Robert seemed so happy in Texas, already had a wonderful job in Dallas and that the family's University Park lifestyle was so comfortable.

After months of trying to save the marriage, the couple separated and Robert moved to an executive apartment in Addison while awaiting his new posting to New York.

Beth had been alerted by the family counselor to be prepared for the worst with Robert Jr., age 17, who was called Bobby, and Sue, age 15. After their Dad moved out, the children seemed to be fine for a while. Of course they were hurt and angry, but Bobby tried to be especially strong and supportive now that he was the "man of the house." Sue became quiet and somewhat withdrawn.

It was several months before the transfer to New York took place. In the final month in Dallas, Robert tried to spend as much time with the children as possible, but he was very busy at work preparing for his transfer. At least, that was what he said when he was late or missed dates to see the children.

Beth learned soon that Robert had met a woman in New York. She didn't know when this had occurred or how long it had been going on. Robert eventually told her that he was planning to move in with this woman. It was now crystal clear that Robert had separated from his old family and that she could expect an unpleasant reaction from both children.

The actual "good-byes" had been painful for all, but it was more than three weeks before Robert called the children from New York. By the time of Robert's call, Bobby and his girlfriend of over a year had broken up and Sue had flunked two quizzes in school.

Also, for the first time in her relationship with her children, Beth had had some disciplinary problems with them. First, Beth learned that Bobby and several other under-18-year-old boys had been stopped by the police for driving erratically. Beth was shocked to hear from the police that Bobby had used a fake I.D. to purchase beer. The driver was charged with driving under the influence and Bobby now had a court date.

Beth called Robert after Bobby was released to his mother's custody from the Carrolton, Texas, police station. Beth could not believe Robert's response as he coldly advised her to call the family lawyer. Beth suggested Robert visit Dallas immediately, but Robert begged off due to the pressure of his new job.

Beth and Bobby managed to handle the legal charges on their own (via a strict warning by the judge), but what had been a strong, loving relationship between mother and son soon deteriorated into a seething, deep, and mutually painful conflict.

At this stage of his life, all should have been good for Bobby. He was in his senior high school year and had already been accepted at Baylor University. Instead, he began to withdraw from contact with his mom. His infrequent telephone conversations with his dad were short and absent the strong fatherly ties the boy wanted.

Bobby's relationship with his sister also showed the strain of the family conflict. They had been very close before their dad left. In spite of the typical adolescent caricature of brother-sister rivalry, Sue and Bobby had always found time for each other. Sue could no longer seem to get Bobby's attention. He always seemed miles away and eventually Sue gave up trying to reach him.

For Sue, the news of her father's departure had been devastating. At first, she did not believe it. He was so special in her life. But when Robert told Sue he was leaving, she believed it, but pleaded for him to stay. He tried to explain that it was not her fault and not even her mother's fault, he just felt he had to go to New York at this point in his life. He assured Sue that he loved her, would see her often and would call weekly.

In fact, Robert's first call to Sue took place three weeks after he had left. His next call was four weeks later. Sue felt abandoned by her father and completely out of communication with her mother. Her withdrawal from family, friends and her excellence in school continued. She began to miss meals and to spend ever more hours alone in her room with her diet sodas, rock music and stuffed animals. Healthy food, schoolwork and her family became neglected memories for this agonized young person.

Conflict between mother and daughter was apparent at virtually every place where their lives crossed. Beth felt there was nothing she could do that would not irritate Sue or drive Bobby further away. It was obviously time for some serious action—or the results could be tragic.

Fortunately for Beth, she had had an undergraduate background in psychology. She had been a day student at Southern Methodist University in Dallas and had retained contact with one of her close college friends, Renee, who now was a clinical psychologist at the SMU Psychology Department clinic. Renee advised family therapy, but getting Bobby and Sue into a program was impossible.

Renee was familiar with the Seven Step program and began coaching Beth in the possibilities for all of them if they would agree to cooperate in the process. The truth is that Beth did most of the initial process work herself.

First, she met with each child and told them to be prepared to be honest about what was on their minds and how they truly saw themselves (Step One). She then assigned each child the task of defining the "problems" currently in his or her life (Step Two).

Beth next asked the children if they were willing to do what it took to resolve their differences, even if it meant some compromise (Step Three). After some days of difficult interplay, the children agreed.

Next, Beth enrolled the children in a process for developing an action plan for possibilities of dealing with what was bothering each (Step Four). This action plan yielded much food for discussion and all three participants agreed to meet not less than once per week for at least one hour to look at the options and evaluate them (Step Five).

In spite of the pain and the barriers to communication, Beth elicited from Bobby and Sue a promise to say what was really on their minds (in a respectful manner) and she agreed to speak about what was troubling her (Step Six).

Finally, after several weeks of family meetings with tough talk, many tears, some shouting and lots of patience from Beth, a plan of action was devised to attempt to get the family functioning again and in a mutually tolerable and healing mode. In celebration, Beth took Bobby and Sue away for a quiet weekend in New Mexico where the three of them learned again to appreciate the special contribution each made in the life of the others (Step Seven).

The case study of Beth and Bobby and Sue shows how even the most complex, family-straining and deeply rooted disputes can be processed by the Seven Steps. There is never a guarantee that they will work, but there is never harm in trying them out.

In this case, the pain was so deep and manifest that something had to be done. A patient mother sought help and was able to facilitate the process into effective action. But, if you asked Beth if it had been easy, you would hear a resounding "no." If you asked her if she felt there was value in the process, she would probably point to the family picture of the three of them taken during their weekend in New Mexico and just smile.

What if the parties to the conflict are children themselves? Can they Iron Out their own differences using the process? The answer is a resounding: YES! the Ironing It

Out process knows no age limits. In fact, children are often quicker to perceive the need for collaborative thinking than their adult counterparts.

Many schools have taken advantage of children's natural instinct to be able to resolve conflicts on their own. School mediation is sometimes referred to as "peer mediation" because it uses the empowerment or facilitation of a fellow student to assist the disputants in working out their problem.

Mediation as a process for nonadversarial resolution has begun to catch on in school systems around the U.S. This process requires a neutral third party. Thus, it differs slightly from the Ironing It Out process, which is designed for the parties themselves; however, it provides a powerful alternative to violence and confrontation so much a part of the school systems of my youth. Additional information about mediation in schools can be obtained through the National Association of Mediation in Education (NAME), which is connected to the University of Massachusetts in Amherst.

For children to learn the Seven Steps, they must first learn a little about the dynamics of conflict—both with their peers and with their parents and other adults. I have presented several exercises to assist in this briefing. See The Young Persons' Exercises 1 through 6 in Section Four.

So, regardless of your age and although it may seem difficult, if not impossible, you too can Iron Out the differences with your parents, children or siblings. You can now see how the steps work. All it takes is the willingness to do it and the commitment to action!

Get going!

OTHER FAMILY DISPUTES

There are a myriad of other family-oriented disputes which could easily fill a separate book. Suffice it to acknowledge that wherever family members are involved in dispute, the sensitivity factors discussed above must come into play.

Two special areas of family conflict deserve some discussion. These are sibling conflicts and family business conflicts.

With siblings, all of the special jealousies, resentments, competition-for-attention factors bump up against the unique sibling love feelings; the result can be conflicts of a particularly painful and vindictive nature. All of us know of at least one family where brothers or sisters haven't spoken to each other for years over some event in the past which might appear trifling to an outsider.

When feelings such as these are in the mix, parties have to be extremely open to a willingness to forgive. Without such willingness, it is unlikely that family disputes can ever really be resolved. If brother A says to brother B, "You're wrong and I am willing to resolve the conflict, but I am not willing to forgive you," is that conflict really resolved?

The answer is clearly: NO. A temporary truce can be in place, but until each is willing to also forgive, the resentment and anger will percolate under the surface until it explodes in another conflict (which, in truth, is probably just a different manifestation of the same old, unresolved conflict).

Another area ripe for conflict is family business. These conflicts are especially difficult because they bring to bear not only the business issues, but also all of the family sensitivity issues discussed above.

All too often, family members who are in conflict fail to look for help soon enough. Results of this delay manifest themselves not only in the business, but also in disastrous family problems.

The Ironing It Out process can work in family business disputes, but it takes careful orchestration by at least one family member who is willing to walk everyone else through it. In these disputes, outside assistance is most often the wisest decision. In the case study which follows, I assisted the family in resolving issues which had festered for at least two generations.

Conflict Case Study

Old man Tomansky had come to the U.S. from Russia with no money and no formal education. He literally started with a pushcart collecting scrap goods in New York and began to build a business in surplus goods. He had six sons. All of the children moved from New York to Connecticut in the early years of this century.

When I came into the case, two of the sons had died with no heirs. Four brothers remained. One was a judge. One was a physician. One was a real estate entrepreneur. The final brother had inherited the family surplus goods business. He also collected and traded in antique automobiles. Each of the other brothers claimed an interest in that business.

All four brothers were approaching their later years and two of the brothers had wives and children. The doctor and judge were unmarried and lived together. The entrepreneur and surplus dealer did not speak to each other and neither of them spoke to the judge or doctor.

Three of the brothers lived in the same small Connecticut city where the family owned a substantial amount of property. The fourth lived in the neighboring city and he too owned substantial property.

These brothers had the financial assets and the will to fight and fight they did!

By the time my law firm was retained to represent the surplus dealer in possible litigation against the other three brothers, the family assets, including property of the two deceased brothers, had been the subject of deep dispute and resentment for years.

My law partners and I decided the best way to bring matters to a head was to initiate a dramatic lawsuit and since our clients had the resources and the inclination to fight, we attacked. I might add, this was long before I had decided to take a more gentle approach to dispute resolution and I had a bit of a reputation for going for the legal throat of my opponent.

Each of the brothers was represented by a large and expensive law firm. The attorney for the doctor and the judge was a senior partner of one of New England's most prestigious firms and was later mentioned for the U.S. Court of Appeals. All four of these brothers were throwing big bucks into this family squabble giving credence to the saying: "A conflict a day keeps the lawyers in pay."

Resolution became possible for the brothers only after everyone was bloodied, embarrassed by the press coverage and realized that the only winners at that point were the lawyers.

The Ironing It Out process was not directly applied at that time (because I had not yet synthesized it as such), but the essence of the breakthrough in reaching a settlement of this hard-fought war was a recognition that each of the steps I have since outlined in this book had to be applied.

It worked and the case settled after a marathon settlement conference that ran more than 15 hours on one day, resumed the second afternoon and went late into that evening.

The Tomansky case dramatically introduced me to the level of emotion, resentment, repressed love and other dynamics of disputes involving family and business.

An important additional note must be added before we leave the discussion of resolving family disputes. Differences between lovers of the same sex, deep long-term friendships, parent-child problems and sibling or intra-family issues all share many of the potentially explosive dynamics. I have chosen a case study arising out of a marriage. I could have chosen to illustrate the process using a conflict arising between long-term lovers, between brothers, or out of a family will contest.

In all of these conflicts, the resolver, whether one of the parties to the dispute or an outsider, must always tread lightly but be prepared to stamp heavily when and where necessary.

The sad thing about the Tomansky case is that all four brothers were financially successful and had nice families, but had fought so long and so hard among themselves that they were chronically unhappy and often clinically depressed. Cousins would not speak to cousins.

From a materialistic standpoint, the Tomansky family was a gold mine to the legal community. My firm litigated several matters for years. Eventually even father and son began to fight. Soon, I found myself pitted against my former law partner as I represented the father and he represented the son, as the Tomansky troubles slipped to a new generation.

Sometime after the original case between the brothers had settled and the father and son began to do battle, I left the practice of law. While my decision had nothing directly to do with this case, it is probably fair to say that this case exemplified the kind of senseless lawyer-assisted combat that factored into my decision to leave the practice of law.

In my former family law practice, I always tried first to see if there could be a peaceful resolution. If I did not think so, it became total war. Perhaps it took the pain of my own marital breakup for me to see these disputes in a new light. One thing is clear, when the dispute involves a family issue, the rules must be tenaciously adhered to and great sensitivity for the feelings of the other side must be present.

The Seven Simple Steps can work well in this category of disputes and have been very effective in many cases of which I am aware. The process is powerful and gets results whether applied by only one side of the conflict or all sides. Naturally, it would be best if all parties would agree to use the steps.

The process is an effective stand-alone tool; however, because of the sensitive nature of these issues, it may be helpful to consider some additional factors when applying the process to the family area:

IRONING IT OUT PROCESS REMINDERS

1. Be certain you know who has agreed to use the steps and that they are fully aware of what each of the Seven Steps requires of them. Lend or buy them a copy of this book.

2. Be certain that there are clearly understood ground rules for how the process will be used by all disputants.

3. Be willing to have it not work. This does not mean that you should give up if the going gets tough, but this process works best when not forced. Your willingness to have it not work will empower it to work!

4. Be understanding of where the other people are with respect to the issues at stake and the process itself.

5. Be gentle. The process works just as effectively (perhaps better) when gently applied as when presented forcefully.

6. Be willing to seek help. Sometimes a third party (a friend, family member or professional) is needed. They can usually assist all parties in carrying out the steps. Be willing to seek the support and be alert to when it might be needed.

The "At Stake" test can help the other party in coming up with the real issues. Feel free to use the sources in this book and elsewhere.

In spite of how difficult family issues are to resolve, you have one wonderful thing going for you: people want to resolve these disputes. No one likes them. So, get the job done. You can do it!

Let's look next at disputes in the Workplace.

15

• •

Workplace Disputes

Among the most irritating and difficult areas of conflict to handle are those disputes which arise at work. Whether between your superior and you or you and one or more fellow workers, a workplace dispute has the power to create deep unhappiness, resentment and poor productivity. This in turn can lead to feelings of frustration, disappointment and loss of self-esteem or poor work performance. Most professional consultants agree that these feelings can lead to illness, loss of work time and sometimes, even violence.

We spend most of our productive, waking time in a workplace environment of some kind. Who wants to go to work where an unpleasant conflict awaits him or her?

In the workplace, disputes take on a new and different meaning from disputes anywhere else. No matter what the issue appears to be, money and cost effectiveness are always *at stake*. No workplace conflict can continue for very long without taking its toll on the health and well-being of the people involved and the workplace itself.

It clearly behooves employer, employee and co-worker to do what each can to Iron Out disputes before they begin to get out of hand.

The process can work effectively in the workplace. It does take commitment by each side to allow it the opportunity to achieve a result. If both sides (or all sides in a group conflict) can agree to use the process, there is a strong likelihood that the conflict will be resolved. Even if only one side (such as you) seems willing (or able) to use the process, it will be far better than doing nothing and . . . it might very well succeed.

To illustrate the point, let's now meet several employees of Clixon Corporation and see how their conflict responded to the Seven Steps.

Conflict Case Study

Charles Hubell, Bill Rangel and Paul Kramer started Clixon over ten years ago. The product was a new type of child safety lock which could keep the youngsters out of closets and drawers.

The business did very well for the first seven years with sales increasing steadily and improved products appearing every so often. Charles, Bill and Paul reaped not only the financial benefits but also the relationship benefits of their hard-fought business struggle. They became even closer friends than they were before they started the company.

Then, something happened.

Bill and his wife Mary Jane were divorced. Bill's new wife, Elizabeth, took an active role in the business. She had a very good business sense and was soon elected to the board of directors. The board now consisted of Charles, Bill, Paul, Elizabeth and Peter (the firm's lawyer).

Elizabeth insisted the company spend more of its revenue on new product research. The rest of the board, except Bill, objected. They warned of tough competition from a new competitor and the need to put the money into advertising. The disagreement became more heated and soon Elizabeth threatened to resign from the board if the rest would not acknowledge her judgment by taking what she felt was essential action to stay ahead of other firms in the field.

*Bill was clearly torn. He knew that the working relation-
ship he had had with Charles and Paul had worked effectively,
yet he was married to Elizabeth and respected her views as both
a business person and wife. She attempted to refrain from influencing his vote, but was pleased when he voted in favor of
her plan.*

*The other directors decided to compromise with Elizabeth
and offered to spend one half of what she had requested as the
research and development budget. She rejected that as "too little
and very possibly, too late." After another week of late meetings and attempts to pacify Elizabeth, Bill showed up one
morning at the office without Elizabeth. "I have her letter of
resignation from the board," he announced to Charles and Paul.*

*Bill had given a portion of his stock in Clixon to Elizabeth
with the knowledge of Charles and Paul. Bill told his partners
and friends how sorry he was that it seemed not to be working
and reluctantly added the news that Elizabeth had seen a lawyer about bringing a shareholder's suit against Charles, Paul and
Peter and even himself, if he remained on the board. Bill resigned.*

*Within a week a letter arrived in Peter's office from an
attorney warning that he was "investigating" a potential shareholder suit by Elizabeth against the corporation. Peter felt he
had to resign from the board now because he couldn't let his
law firm be at risk even though he felt Elizabeth had no legal
leg to stand on and he was sorry to see the business in disarray at the top.*

*Neither Charles nor Paul could concentrate well on business
and sales began to fall. Something had to be done and quickly!*

*Peter told Charles and Paul about the Ironing It Out pro-
cess and both agreed to see if it could help resolve a conflict
which threatened the very future of an outstanding business.
Elizabeth and Bill were invited by Charles and Paul to participate in the Ironing It Out process. They agreed.*

*The first step in the process is to remove all masks. In this
case, it meant each party to the dispute looking inside to who
he or she really was and being willing to be honest about what
persona was coming to the conflict.*

*Charles and Paul soon saw that in addition to being cor-
porate executives and founders of the firm, they were men and*

were bringing with them a prejudgment about women in senior management roles. Bill saw that he was bringing not only his position as a founder of the firm, but also the marital dynamic with all of its nuances. Elizabeth acknowledged that she was bringing some past anger at lack of respect for her in a prior position. She also saw herself as Bill's wife and partner.

Next, Charles, Paul, Bill and Elizabeth agreed to search for the real problem (Step Two). Each had his/her own version of what was really going on. Elizabeth felt that she was being rejected because of her newness in the organization and the fact that she was a female. The men felt that Elizabeth was being overly aggressive and was too new.

After much lively discussion, it emerged that the real problem was the potential loss of market share to competitors in the field. All agreed that that was the real issue and that the dynamic of the relatively recent arrival of Elizabeth was a secondary issue.

Having ascertained the real issue, the group could then go on to consideration of giving up the "must-win" position each held (Step Three). In this case, that manifested itself in a willingness to consider the plan of the other and being open to more than one solution. This led immediately and naturally to Step Four (Development of Several Possible Solutions). In this step, each person devised three possibilities and rated them from their own first choice down to the minimum they each could live with.

Everyone shared the developed options with the others for evaluation (Step Five). The evaluation process occurred on both a group and individual level.

Among the choices presented as "finalists" for consideration by everyone were:

a. Elizabeth return and a smaller research and development budget be enacted.

b. The company consider licensing its technology and operate as a holding company to distribute royalties.

c. Money be spent on research and development with Elizabeth as an outside consultant supervising the project.

It is interesting to note that several of these choices/possibilities didn't even exist in the minds of everyone until it was presented in a creative problem-solving environment.

Step Five suggests that one of the choices be selected and then effectively communicated to each of the other parties to the conflict (Step Six). Since effective communication means delivery in a manner designed to be received (which implies the other side must be willing to listen or "get it"), all parties set up a process within the process for communicating his/her choice among the three finalists. In this case, the selection of choices was written and individually delivered by each party to the others with an agreement that each had ten uninterrupted minutes to explain their selection of alternative.

After additional lively discussion following this elaborate communication process, everyone agreed that it was best for the company to wind up its operations, but that the technology had strong value and Elizabeth was selected to lead a search for a place to license the know-how for royalties. She would then present the proposed deal to the remaining board members, who now again included Bill. The board would negotiate a deal through Peter and would cease active operations. It would continue to exist as a legal vehicle to distribute royalties to shareholders.

As it turned out, Charles and Paul also had reached a point in their lives where they felt it was time to look at other projects. This conflict had actually presented each person with an opportunity to break into something new which interested them. Seeing this for themselves, Charles, Paul, Bill and Elizabeth were ready to acknowledge each other (Step Seven) for his/her contribution to the others and to express readily appreciation for the value in the relationship. Issues of tension and discomfort between Charles and Paul on the one hand and Elizabeth and Bill on the other were eliminated. The relationship between Bill and Elizabeth also benefited from the process.

A difficult and seemingly overwhelming business crisis was averted in the example above. The matter called for new and creative thinking. Resolution became possible when the attitude shifted from adversarial (must-win) positions to mutual problem solving (partnership for results).

The Ironing It Out process is not necessarily easy. This is especially true where more than two parties are involved. But it works.

Where disputes arise in a workplace environment between only two people, the process offers a somewhat easier approach. There is an easier pattern to follow in walking the steps because other people are not present to complicate matters. Even with only two parties, resolving conflicts using the Seven Simple Steps takes work and commitment.

Even though Ironing Out conflicts is not easy, when compared to the financial cost, business down time, emotional drain and other negative factors, resolving conflicts is a far better business choice than the alternatives. Further, in the workplace very often the dispute can represent a serious, if not fatal threat to the very existence of the firm and unresolved conflict can lead to dangerous, violent confrontation.

Professor Richard Balnave of the University of Virginia School of Law points out the danger of a company's technology becoming obsolete while the company plods slowly through the legal process.[23] Professor Eric Green of Boston University School of Law agrees. Many of the disputes being handled by his own private mediation firm result from business problems which could threaten the existence or financial well-being of the organization in conflict.[24]

In his landmark book, *Managing For Results*[25], Peter Drucker discusses the creative importance of disagreements in the business environment. Uncertainties and ambiguities are key elements to Professor Drucker; however, they don't live alone, but rather in a process of discovery and resolution-seeking with a goal of reaching better business decisions in the organization at the highest level. The corollary to that would also be true; if decisions cannot be reached at the highest level, disagreement could be a very destructive force in the business.

One of the best-selling leadership books in recent years talks about "win/win" thinking. Stephen R. Covey sees win/win as a philosophy of living.[26] This cooperative attitude is not the result of normal development processes for most people, according to Covey. It has to be learned. In fact, Covey refers to this shift in attitude as one of his "powerful lessons in personal change." No one can argue with Covey's premise because the results of shifts in thinking from competition to cooperation are manifest in the workplace.

It probably can be said that the Quality Improvement Movement which is now so "hot" in U.S. business and which helped catapult Japan into world economic leadership builds upon a framework of cooperative thinking in the workplace. This is not to say that conflict won't exist or, as Drucker points out, does not have a place in decision making.

Various other sources can be cited for the proposition that conflict can destroy a business faster than almost anything else. If that is true, the object then is to deal with the forces of disagreement and conflict in a powerful and creative way. The Seven Simple Steps offer that possibility.

How grievances are dealt with in the workplace is an indicator of how committed the organization is to cooperative or collaborative thinking and peaceful resolution of disputes. A. L. Williams and Associates is a nationwide life insurance and financial services marketing organization with thousands of independent agents and managers in all 50 states. Under the guidance of its then Corporate Counsel Judy Cohn, A. L. Williams developed an in-house dispute resolution system which resolved most issues before they reached a sufficient level of conflict to end up in litigation.

The A. L. Williams program was the first of its kind in the United Stated and continues successfully today. It has virtually eliminated litigation in an area which is filled with lawsuits. The A. L. Williams program has been described in greater detail in an article by Ms. Cohn and Adam J. Conti.[27]

As an employer or worker, you don't need an elaborate program to assist in seeing that conflicts are worked out fairly. Sometimes, the Ironing It Out process can be incorporated in whole or part into a firm's grievance procedure. In the materials in Section Four, there is a draft grievance procedure clause. I designed this clause for a small, very closely knit firm in the health care field. That firm was committed to Ironing Out conflicts, if possible, before they erupted into illness, legal trouble or workplace downtime.

Sometimes, as with other disputes discussed in this book, outside help is needed. Mediation is an excellent medium for resolving business conflicts without destroying relationships. In fact, the federal government and many other private and public sector organizations are using mediation to resolve all manner of workplace disputes. My firm has led mediation training programs for EEO, disabilities and other workplace disputes. Industrial psychology can assist powerfully in many cases as can organizational behavior consulting where appropriate.

Some resource suggestions for assistance in resolving business and workplace conflicts are listed in Section Four of the book.

16

●●

Public Disputes

Most of the conflicts described in this book so far have dealt with very personal and, in some cases, very private issues. Even business or commercial disputes are considered private in that they don't usually involve a public agency or some communitywide situation.

What if the conflict does involve public issues in some way?

Would the Ironing It Out process apply?

Can you actually affect policy in some way using this process?

I am pleased to tell you that the Ironing It Out process is very powerful in the public-dispute arena, although there are many auxiliary factors that have to be considered.

First of all, let's decide what we mean by the term "public disputes." As with many of the other terms in this field, public disputes have been variously described by a number of commentators. These disputes are often the meat of juicy news accounts. Names like "Love Canal," "Three Mile Island," "Chernobyl," "Bhopal," "Bosnia-Herzegovina," "Somalia," and "Exxon Valdez" are the stuff of headlines. And clearly these tragedies involved public disputes; but lesser known issues such as what is happening to the zoning laws in your neighborhood or who is polluting your nearby river or why the school board is cutting teacher salaries also involve public disputes—on a very personal level.

So, for our purposes, we shall consider a public dispute to be any issue or conflict which involves two or more persons and which has impact directly or indirectly on the community or any segment of it.

Now, if you think you are not involved in public disputes or have no influence over their outcome you are probably right—at least as far as their outcome. You are certainly involved in them whether you like it or not. But if, on the other hand, you feel strongly about things going on around you and how they impact you and others, you are ready to tackle the public dispute arena.

Professor Larry Susskind and Jeffrey Cruikshank have written a marvelous book on "consensual approaches to resolving public disputes." *Breaking The Impasse*[28] may be to public disputes what *Getting To Yes* is to negotiation. This book is heartily recommended for serious students of the field and should be helpful to those interested in the dynamics and fabric of these kinds of issues.

To Susskind and Cruikshank, public disputes engender a very specific process for development of collaborative approaches to problem solving. The process is made up of distinct phases or stages ("prenegotiation, negotiation and initiation").

Their point seems very valid for the issues which confront a number of people and have long-term impact on a group. They are also addressed to issues with many players. In fact, in my own experience with group conflict, I have observed that success in resolution can only come when a well-thought-out, staged approach is used.

The Ironing It Out process can offer a staged program also. If one looks at the Seven Steps (Section Two), one can see how they can fit into stages of prenegotiation, negotiation and implementation. But, the process is designed primarily to assist in the negotiation phase. In truth, it is in that stage where many disputes, public and private, are resolved.

Let's take a look now at a public dispute case study and see what effect the Ironing It Out process had.

Conflict Case Study

Blair purchased an old school building on the outskirts of the city on a main road which he thought would make an ideal bed and breakfast establishment. The area was zoned for an inn, but not a public restaurant, so Blair approached the neighbors about their feelings regarding a possible zoning variance to have a public eating facility in their part of town. Blair was a very flamboyant personality who intended to name the restaurant "Blair House."

When word got around about Blair's plans, several neighbors from the street behind the old school banded together to try to block the proposed zoning change. This group threatened a court injunction if the gaudy entrepreneur proceeded with his plans.

Fortunately for Blair, his attorney knew about the Seven Simple Steps and advised his client to consider an Ironing It Out approach. Blair thought about the steps and sought counsel from a business adviser friend on how to present the steps and himself to the opposition.

The first thing his adviser suggested was that Blair remove all the gaudiness and frills both from himself and from the plan (Step One). Next, she suggested that Blair ask himself what he really wanted from these people—in other words, find out what the real problem was (Step Two).

Blair had told the neighborhood group that he was prepared to fight a court battle with them if necessary because of all the money he already had tied up in the project. His adviser suggested a more conciliatory approach (Step Three) and that the parties meet at the proposed site. Blair was given a homework assignment with his attorney and builder: to develop several possible alternative plans (Step Four) and be prepared to select one (Step Five).

Blair knew that communication was a key (Step Six), so he personally visited every household in the neighborhood which had opposed his plan and invited the residents to attend a meeting at the old school. Blair dressed conservatively, was relaxed and truly himself (i.e., no mask or pretension) when he spoke. He made a very effective presentation and invited creative thinking from the group.

The result was a revised plan for the building and site which included a smaller, exclusive restaurant open to the general public only on weekends. Blair invited the attendees and their families to a special private dinner at the new inn just before it opened and thanked them for their support (Step Seven).

The process in Blair's case assisted him in coming up with a better plan for the site than he originally had and led to a nice continuing relationship with the neighbors, many of whom became regular weekend diners.

You may wonder whether or not this was a "public" dispute, but in fact, unless something was done to Iron Out the situation, a neighborhood lawsuit and counterclaims were inevitable. Because of the personality of Blair and the expensive homes in the area, the press followed this matter keenly. By Ironing Out the problem, further public comment and scrutiny were preempted.

In those dramatic "true" public disputes where whole cities, regions and sometimes even countries are involved, resolution of disputes is only reached by building consensus in looking for answers. When one side tries to impose its will on the other, disaster is inevitable.

My colleague and friend, attorney Charles Lancaster, was assistant program director for ADR on the staff of the U.S. Army Corps of Engineers. In environmental and other land-use disputes, according to Lancaster, consensus building is the true challenge for the developer (whether public such as the Corps of Engineers or private such as a builder). The goal is to enroll neighbors and other members of the community in the planned event. A relatively new term, "partnering," has been created to describe early planning for disposition of conflict which may involve groups or the public in general.

An important point relevant to discussion of public conflicts is the delineation between "group" conflict and "public" conflict. By definition, it can be said that a group conflict is one which involves three or more people and which pertains to the various interests of individuals within the group. By contrast, a public dispute may involve a number of people also, but has at its core one or more issues which in some fashion affect the public.

Notwithstanding whether or not the dispute is a group or public one, whenever it involves large numbers of people, the issues must be broken down into manageable pieces before there can be attempts at resolution.

The first step, even before the Seven Simple Steps can be considered, is to find out who the decision makers are and how to communicate with them effectively. This is an essential step in breaking the conflict down into pieces which can be moved toward resolution. This is by no means an easy task and involves many other skills related to group dynamics.

While I do not know of any instance where my specific delineation of the Seven Steps has been formally (or informally) used as part of the public consensus-building program for a major public project, I can state without question that the process steps would work very well. I can also assume that steps like these are undertaken every day in these kinds of disputes.

When you see a public dispute (or are part of one), feel free to share your knowledge of the Ironing It Out process with others.

The results may be dramatic.

17

• •

All Those Other Disputes

I stated in the early pages of this book that I would not presume to be able to cover each and every type of conflict one might expect to come upon if one is living a normal life. Now that you have completed the last few chapters, you will see that that is true, but that doesn't mean there isn't a way for dealing with these other disputes.

What kind of disputes do I mean? They can range from an argument with a mechanic over the work done to a shouting match on the highway with a crazy driver to frustration and disappointment with the government over the way they are handling a problem of yours.

So, what do you do when a dispute comes along that doesn't seem to fit into any of the categories covered in this book or is a variation from the example?

What happens when something unpleasant confronts you which you have never heard about or read about before?

The answer to these questions lies with trust. By that I mean trust in yourself and the basic premises of human behavior that drive us all. Remember Basic Point No. 4 that conflict is a normal part of life and Basic Point No. 9 that humans want and need to communicate with each other—they *want* to resolve the conflicts even through it does not always look that way at first.

I never promised that I would turn you into an expert in conflict resolution. I did promise that I would present some tools which can afford you the chance to see how you can shift the conflict from a negative to a positive (see Chapter 18) and how you work through the upset using the Seven Simple Steps.

These steps have been purposefully formulated in a very generic way—so they can apply to virtually all conflicts you face. It is up to you to analyze the problem at hand to see if and how the steps can apply to a given situation. I can't do that for you (although that is much of what I do in my mediation practice).

I'm sorry to say it: The Buck Stops With You! (Of course, you knew that all along and maybe that was part of your motivation in buying this book). So, if the "buck" (the problem) is in your hands, please follow some of the analytical thoughts, processes and forms in this book, know the answer is in your mind and trust that you will do the right thing.

If you feel you are not sufficiently in control of the situation to apply the Ironing It Out process, see if you can reasonably get control. If you can (and the steps might help you get there), got to work. If you can't reasonably get control, it may be time to get some help at least in equalizing control factors. This help can come from any third party who can be objective enough not to take on either side or it can come from a professional.

Please note that I used the term "reasonable" when talking about control above. That does not mean the use of force, violence, undue pressure or other duress. It means getting the attention of the other side and the commitment to at least listen to what you have to say. If they attempt to use such pressure tactics on you, it is definitely time for outside assistance. You will note how many times in the case studies it was a third party who provided some initial assistance in applying the process.

The Seven Simple Steps can work well in almost any category of dispute and have been very effective in many cases of which I am aware. The process is powerful and gets results whether applied by only one side of the conflict or all sides. Naturally, it would be best if all parties would agree to use the steps.

As stated earlier, in spite of how difficult some of the issues are to resolve, you have one wonderful thing going for you: people want to resolve them.

It does take a commitment to see conflict as presenting opportunity. For more information about how conflict can show up as opportunity, read on.

18

• •

Conflict as Opportunity

In the early pages of this book, I referred to the many courses, seminars and materials about "self-actualization" or "self-discovery" now offered by the vendors of what I call "auto-identity." I will admit, for the record, that I have taken several of these courses, reluctantly at first, then with a bit more enthusiasm. I began to see the power in learning about myself first in order to be able to work with or teach others.

One of the gifts I took away from my participation in The Forum[29] was a new way to look at the difficult things in my life. Forum graduates are taught to see *breakdown* as an *opportunity.* Breakdown in this context can be loosely defined as any upset or failure in peoples' expectations of themselves, others or situations in their lives. This simple change in the way I look at the disappointments in my life has transformed my entire personal approach to life—with very positive results.

Because conflicts often manifest themselves in breakdown, a similar result is possible in the area of conflict.

Changing the way you see conflict has the potential to change much about the way you see your life and certainly can make your dealing with conflict a manageable, even creative process. The very purpose for the Ironing It Out process is to offer an opportunity to master conflict.

Seeing the opportunity in breakdown or difficulty is an essential step in transforming the nightmare of conflict into the awakening of resolution.

When confronted by a challenging situation, sometimes the worst parts of our beings show themselves. We often live in our reactions to situations rather than acting to handle these difficulties.

One reason we are like this, as Dr. Michael Mahoney says, is that we become extremely self-conscious about our abilities at difficult times. He reasons that all the negative attention and criticism which has been part of our lives since early childhood finally takes its toll at the time of trouble: "By the time we are adults we are not only well-trained self-critics, but we may have come to believe that our negative self-evaluations are true."[30]

It won't be possible to see conflict as opportunity or accomplish much else in your life until you have a mechanism in place with which to process built-in self-negative thoughts. To Dr. Mahoney, self-awareness, while helpful, is not enough. He sees the need for affirmative action to counter feelings of despair, inadequacy or helplessness. The Seven Steps of the Ironing It Out process can be that mechanism in appropriate cases.

When I think of negative thoughts, I recall the classic story told by Dr. Denis Waitley[31] about a famous game of the World Series. It was the bottom of the ninth inning. The Braves were leading the Yankees and could win, if only pitcher Warren Spahn could strike out Yankee batter Elston Howard.

The Braves manager went to the mound and told pitcher Spahn what *not* to throw. You can guess what happened next. He threw the pitch he wasn't supposed to, Howard hit it and the Yankees won.

This story illustrates a classic example of the creation of negative possibilities. We seem to do this to ourselves all the time. Of course, these automatic negative thoughts reinforce all the negative programming we have received since our early childhood days.

As we look at the challenge of a conflict situation or any other difficult situation in our lives, there is a temptation to automatically use expressions such as "why bother," "it will never work," or "this is a waste of time, but . . ."

Each one of these kinds of expressions creates a potential for self-fulfilling prophesy. That is not to say that we should rush blindly into every situation without careful, even occasionally negative evaluation. Dangerous situations which require restraint and self-doubt when needed can save us from disaster (e.g., "Look before you leap"). That is why the process asks you to develop several possible courses of action (Step Four).

We should not always look for perfection in our reactions to difficult situations. As Dr. Mahoney points out, not only does that create an impossible situation for us, the search itself can be counter-productive. Instead, we should look for effective solutions, which are those "which change the appropriate situation, behavior or thought pattern."[32]

Looking at problems, including conflicts, with a view to what is positive in them—what you can learn—where you can go—has the ability to transform the thought patterns and thus assist in solving the problems.

You could quickly learn the Seven Simple Steps and even put them into practice without trying to transform your perception of the conflict. But, in my view, you would be cheating yourself. If, in fact, conflict is part of human development, as we learned in Section One, and is normal and even necessary for education and advancement through life, then why not see the opportunity in conflict and learn to maximize the potential in the situation?

Throughout this book I have asked you to alter the ways you view certain things. Thus, when I say you should see conflict as opportunity, my words may sound glib and simplistic. I know this change is not easy. No one expects you to unlearn all the negative thoughts you, as a human being, have accumulated over the years.

I can only expect you to approach this proposition with the same objectivity with which you have approached other suggestions in this book. I can also offer some helpful hints in learning how to see *conflict* as *opportunity*.

The questions posed in the short test below will force you to evaluate the potential benefits and detriments of a conflict situation.

THE CONFLICT/OPPORTUNITY TEST

1. What is the conflict (where and how does it manifest itself)?

2. Who are the players in this conflict drama (and how do they relate to you)?

3. If this conflict is resolved, what are the benefits?

4. If this conflict is not resolved, is there a payoff in some way for me?

5. If this conflict is not resolved, what harm can follow?

6. If this conflict is resolved, will the benefit create a better situation than before the conflict arose?

7. Whatever the outcome, can I see that the conflict added a positive dimension to the potential outcome?

If you have looked at these questions and given them fair, honest appraisal and objective answers, I would predict that the answer to Question 7 would be "yes." If that is the case, you will have seen the *opportunity* which lives within conflict.

Without taking away any of the benefits of the actual conflict resolution steps outlined in Section Two of this book, I would consider my job done well as the author of a book on conflict resolution if you can begin to see that merely transforming the way you look at conflict (from "breakdown" to "opportunity") can be a powerful tool in your life.

One of the best ways to put the transformed approach to conflict into practice is in the way you use language. Try to be mindful of how you say things and watch for those self-fulfilling negative possibilities.

Change the "it's impossible" thoughts to "what an opportunity" thoughts . . . and watch what happens! Combine this new positive internal and external languaging with your use of the Seven Steps and you are well on your way to being able to Iron Out unpleasant conflicts or, said in another way: personal mastery of conflict.

On this positive note and with great confidence in your commitment to making life better for you and those around you, I end the instructional portion of the text.

What follows in Section Four are some forms and resources for you to use when things get tough.

Thanks for being my partner on this journey toward making yourself and this planet just a little better by the removal of unpleasant, debilitating, negative conflict.

four

Forms and Resources

"Conflict is to reality what hot fudge is to ice cream; it may melt a little away, but it adds to the overall flavor."
—Anonymous

19

•••

Terms and Forms

The forms in this chapter are presented as accessories to the Ironing It Out process. To assist in understanding the forms and as a resource for the entire book, I have presented first a concise glossary of some of the more common terms used in the field of conflict or dispute resolution. These are my definitions and they are intentionally not presented in "legalese" or "psychologese." If more detailed definitions are needed, check the Resources List in Chapter 20.

GLOSSARY OF TERMS

ACCORD—an agreement.

ADR—the abbreviation for the term Alternative Dispute Resolution. This is the generally accepted term in the legal and professional dispute resolution community; although the latter prefer simply: "Dispute Resolution."

ADJUDICATION—the process of going forward in the traditional court system to obtain a judgment on the merits of an issue.

AGREEMENT—the outcome of a successful discussion, negotiation or other process which represents the meeting of the minds of the parties with respect to the subject matter. It may be oral or in writing and is usually binding unless expressed otherwise.

ARBITRATION—the process whereby a neutral third person is designated by parties in a dispute to hear the issue and render a decision. The parties may decide in advance whether or not that decision will be binding. Arbitration is considered an ADR procedure, although it is presented in an adversarial forum.

BINDING—the agreement of the parties to give full legal effect to their outcome.

COLLABORATION—the process of reaching agreement by satisfaction of mutual goals, i.e., a "win-win" solution.

CONCILIATION—the process where a neutral third party assists disputants in resolving a dispute by direct discussion with each, not usually in the presence of the other(s) (i.e., "shuttle diplomacy"). It is often likened to counseling in dealing with disputes except the goal is to assist parties in resolving their differences. It is considered by many as an ADR process and is often confused with mediation.

COUNSELING—the process conducted by a fully qualified and licensed professional (e.g., attorney or mental health provider) designed to assist the party or parties in dealing with their situation in some fashion. It is not necessarily geared to resolving disputes. It is not an ADR process.

COURT-ANNEXED—in certain jurisdictions, there is an ADR program (either arbitration or mediation) which is connected to the court system. This means that judges will refer matters to the court's own ADR system (if they have one) or to private or community organizations.

COMMUNITY MEDIATION—the term refers to mediation centers with a community base or mission. These are usually non-profit organizations using trained volunteer mediators.

CONFLICT—any disagreement or dispute or other issue which forces a choice upon a person. See Chapters 2 through 5.

DISPUTANTS—the parties who are engaged in a process to resolve their dispute.

FACILITATION—a general term used whenever a third party assists others in reaching mutually established goals.

IMPASSE—that point in a discussion, negotiation or mediation when it becomes apparent that parties are unwilling or unable to come to agreement.

MED-ARB—a relatively new concept in ADR where the mediation process is thoroughly explored first and, if it proves unsuccessful, the mediator is then authorized by the parties to act as an arbitrator and render a decision.

MEDIATION—the process whereby a neutral third party selected by the disputants assists them in reaching accord through distinct procedural steps designed to develop agreement. The parties set the ground rules and may agree to be bound or not. It is a recognized ADR process achieving ever-increasing support.

NEGOTIATION—a term used to describe active and committed discussion designed to reach specific goals.

OMBUDSPERSON—a person usually designated by an organization to function in a so-called neutral capacity to assist people in dealing with that organization.

PRIVATE OR RENT-A-JUDGE—the process of hiring a person (usually a retired judge) to deal with the dispute. Most often this results in an arbitration.

PUBLIC DISPUTE—a dispute or problem which affects directly or indirectly a large group, community or segment of society.

SETTLEMENT—an agreement which represents the successful outcome of a discussion, negotiation or ADR process and which ends the dispute.

THE FORMS

It should be noted that each situation is unique and probably requires its own variation of the standard form supplied here. However, I hope these forms can provide some guidance and a starting point in your design of a mechanism to assist in bringing the other side to the table and in resolving your home, business, family or workplace conflict.

Another caveat is in order: Some of these forms may seem to be legal documents and, in fact, when used properly, they can have sound legal effect; however, just as this book is not designed to be a substitute for legal or other professional advice, neither are the forms designed to replace the need to seek professional counsel when necessary.

List of Forms

1. Seven Steps Checklist
2. Conflict Issue Checklist/Questionnaire
3. The "At Stake" Questionnaire
4. Sample Request to Negotiate (Iron It Out)
5. Sample Resolution Understanding
6. Sample Mediation Clause
7. Sample Mediation Agreement
8. Sample Company Dispute Resolution Policy
9. Sample Company Grievance Procedure

Index to Exercises

Young Persons' Exercise 1, The Tree House

Young Persons' Exercise 2, The Candy Game

Young Persons' Exercise 3, The Animal Conflict Game

Young Persons' Exercise 4, Thought Provocation About Conflict

Young Persons' Exercise 5, The Seven Simple Steps

Young Persons' Exercise 6, The Dispute Detective

Form 1

The following checklist should act as a reminder and support tool to assist in following the Seven Steps in an orderly fashion:

The Problem (Conflict):

The Steps:

☐ **1.** Have I removed all of my masks? Am I being honest and authentic in my handling and approach to this conflict?

☐ **2.** Have I looked for and discovered the *real* problem or am I being distracted by apparent issues which are getting in the way?

☐ **3.** Am I willing to not "win"? Would I accept something less than total victory? Could I compromise?

☐ **4.** Have I looked at more than one possible outcome for this issue? Am I willing to develop several options?

☐ **5.** Have I fully evaluated the options/possibilities and come up with a workable choice?

☐ **6.** Have I communicated my choice and the reasons in an effective way? Has my communication been received?

☐ **7.** Have I expressed my appreciation for the hard work put in by the other side to resolve this issue? Have I expressed my appreciation for the value I have in my relationship with the other side?

What else do I have to do to work this out?

CONFLICT ISSUE CHECKLIST/QUESTIONNAIRE

Form 2

1. Parties to the dispute:

    a. _____

    b. _____

2. When did the dispute arise? _____

_____

3. How was it first noticed (and by whom)? _____

_____

4. Nature of the dispute (summary of the problem):

    a. General description: _____

_____

    b. Specific point(s)

1.	5.	9.
2.	6.	10.
3.	7.	11.
4.	8.	12.

5. The Bottom Line (top five points in the problem):

_____

_____

_____

_____

_____

6. Is there any area of potential agreement foreseen (or possible)?

_____

_____

7. Where is there area for "give"?

_____

_____

8. Action(s) taken to date:

_____

_____

9. Timeline(s):   Date: What happened:

_____

_____

10. Action(s) *to be taken* (try to prioritize the steps and number them):

    1. _____

    2. _____

    3. _____

11. Areas where outside assistance is/may be needed:

_____

_____

12. Resources for outside assistance:

_____

_____

THE "AT STAKE" QUESTIONNAIRE

Form 3

1. Ask yourself what the other side has at stake here.

2. Ask yourself what you have at stake here.

3. Ask if these "at stake" issues are totally incompatible.

4. If they are not incompatible, look for mutuality of interest.

5. If they are incompatible, look for a basis for resolution not inconsistent with either your or the other side's "at stake" issues."

6. If you cannot come up with any possibilities for either 4 or 5 above, seek the advice of a third party to assist you with answers to this test regarding the conflict.

7. If, after talking with a third party, the two of you cannot come up with any possibilities for 4 or 5 above, it is time to seek professional conflict resolution assistance. (A listing of some sources is located in Chapter 20.)

SAMPLE REQUEST TO NEGOTIATE (IRON IT OUT)

Form 4

(In letter form to be addressed to the other side of the dispute)

To:

I want you to know that I am committed to Ironing Out our differences.

I want you to know that I am prepared to re-think the issues if that is what it takes to resolve matters with you.

I want you to know that I value our relationship and am confident that we can work this out in a fair and reasonable manner.

I invite you to meet with me (talk to me/write to me) to discuss this and I ask only that you bring the same commitment I have to reaching a resolution.

Thank you for considering this request for discussion.

Note: This form can become the basis not only of a written invitation to communicate, but also of a telephone or personal conversation. If the sincerity and commitment to Iron It Out can be heard by the other side, they probably will agree to "come to the table."

SAMPLE RESOLUTION UNDERSTANDING

Form 5

We acknowledge that we have had a misunderstanding about:

We further acknowledge that we wish to resolve this misunderstanding.

This writing will evidence the fact that after careful discussion, all sides being fully heard and considered, we have reached an understanding as follows:

It is (is not) our intention for this understanding to become a binding legal document. (If you desire a legally binding agreement add the following: The consideration for this agreement is the mutual exchange of the promises outlined.)

This understanding is signed by us on this _____ day of _____ 19 __ freely and after full consideration by each. By signing this voluntarily, each signer commits to carry out the intention of this understanding.

Witness:

_____

Note: It is probably a good idea to have a third party as a witness even if this understanding is nothing more than a good faith expression of good will and is not intended to be a binding contract.

SAMPLE MEDIATION CLAUSE

Form 6

The undersigned, in consideration of the exchange of mutual promises, hereby agree to submit to mediation the following issue(s):

It is further agreed that each party will attend at least one working session with a neutral mediator agreed upon within two weeks of notification of an available date by the mediator. Further, each party agrees that he/she will come to the table with full authority and a willingness to settle all matters in dispute.

Each party agrees to contribute equally to the costs of mediation (unless one side agrees to pay all of the costs).

Each party fully understands that he/she retains all legal rights and powers to proceed to any other remedy at law or equity if the mediation session(s) does not produce an agreement acceptable to each.

The Mediator designated is: _____

This agreement to mediate is (is not) a binding agreement and each party agrees to take no further action until after the mediation session is held.

Signed at: _____   Date: _____

_____

_____

SAMPLE MEDIATION AGREEMENT

Form 7

(To be included in any agreement)

The parties agree that any controversy arising out of this agreement or any interpretation of this agreement which they are not able to resolve themselves shall be submitted to mediation before any other legal action is taken. The parties agree that _____ shall be the mediator (or such other mediator as the parties may agree upon). Costs and expenses of the mediation shall be borne equally by the parties. Mediation shall take place within two weeks after notification by the aggrieved party of a request for mediation unless extended by the mediator. If the mediation does not result in an agreement acceptable to all sides, each may take such other action as he/she/it deems advisable under law or equity. In the event any party takes such legal action without first submitting the issue(s) to mediation as required by this clause, the moving party shall pay the legal expenses of the responding party plus all court costs incurred by said action.

Note: This clause may be inserted into existing agreements, by amendment or modification as provided for in the agreement. It may be utilized in new or pending agreements by giving a copy to counsel with instructions to include this type of clause or by placing it into the agreement yourself. Obviously, this is a generic clause and may not be suitable to your situation. Different situations require different clauses. A collection of mediation clauses is available from the author.

SAMPLE COMPANY DISPUTE RESOLUTION POLICY

Form 8

Subject: Alternative Dispute Resolution

This organization recognizes that for many business disputes there is a less expensive, easier to handle, more effective method of resolution than the traditional legal process. Alternative Dispute Resolution (ADR) procedures involve techniques which can often spare businesses the high cost and adverse impact of litigation.

In recognition of the foregoing, this firm subscribes to the following statement of principle on behalf of our company and its subsidiaries:

> In the event of a business dispute between our company and another company we are committed to exploring with that other party resolution of the dispute through direct negotiation or ADR techniques in good faith before pursuing full-scale litigation. If either our company or the other party believes that the dispute is not suitable for ADR techniques, or if such techniques do not produce results satisfactory to the disputants, either party may proceed with litigation.

In all relationships both within and without this firm, this Policy Statement should be borne in mind.

Chief Executive Officer

Date

Source for this form:
   The above draft policy statement is based upon a proposal to companies by CPR Dispute Resolution (CPR), 680 Fifth Avenue, New York, NY 10019.
   If your firm executes a form such as this, a copy of the policy statement may be sent to CPR at the address above and/or to Mediate-Tech, Inc., P.O. Box 607 Front Royal, VA 22630, both of whom maintain registries of companies who have agreed to resolve disputes through ADR and provide dispute resolvers.

SAMPLE COMPANY GRIEVANCE PROCEDURE

Form 9

VII. EMPLOYEE GRIEVANCES

It is the intention of this firm to provide a safe, comfortable working environment and fair treatment of employees. As part of this fair treatment, this firm is committed to the resolution of employee grievances in a reasonable manner. Employees understand that the following procedure regarding the disposition of disputes arising out of the employment relationship is mandatory.

1. In the event of a dispute between the employee and this firm, or an employee and another employee or party acting as agent for this firm, the aggrieved employee shall first attempt to resolve the issue by direct discussion with his/her supervisor or the other party.

2. If the direct discussion outlined above does not resolve the complaint, the aggrieved employee shall next formally notify his/her supervisor of the grievance. The supervisor shall investigate the complaint promptly (within two working days unless there are extenuating circumstances such as business travel). The supervisor shall issue a report on the grievance to both the employee and the general manager. The report may be oral or written, at the discretion of the supervisor. The report shall contain a recommended disposition of the complaint.

3. If an employee feels his/her supervisor has been unfair in any manner in the conducting of the investigation or that the employee wishes further action of the complaint, he/she must then request investigation of the grievance by a manager or other person not his or her supervisor who also has two days to investigate and report results to both the employee and office manager (unless the general manager is the investigating person, in which case results of the report shall be passed to the employee and the President or his designee).

4. If the second report and recommendation referred to above does not resolve the employee's complaint, the issue shall be referred to a resolution process through a neutral person not involved in any way with the dispute. This person may be an employee of this firm or not. The neutral party shall attempt a reconciliation and/or resolution of the dispute by conciliation between this firm and the employee or the employees in dispute within five working days of the second investigation and report as referred to above. If conciliation does not yield a positive result, the issue shall be submitted to mediation through a neutral mediator designated by this firm and agreed to by the employee. The mediation shall take place within three working days of the neutral's report subject to the mediator's schedule. This firm shall pay for the mediation.

5. In the event the grievance process outlined above does not yield an acceptable disposition of the grievance for the employee, the employee shall then have any and all other options at law and equity as he/she deems appropriate under the circumstances.

Accepted by:

_____

Employee

Date:

_____

Witnessed By:

_____

For the Firm

YOUNG PERSON'S EXERCISE 1

The Tree House

What follows is a simple but powerful exercise in learning about conflict and resolution for children. It encourages them to be able to empathize with the conflict experience.

This exercise is performed by: (1) telling the participants the following story (fact situation), (2) asking the participants to answer the questions following the story and (3) discussing with the participants how it must feel to be each of the people.

Story: *Jan and Pete and Pam were friends. Jan lived next door to Pete and Pam who were brother and sister. Pete and Pam's dad, Mr. Parsons, agreed to build a tree house in a tree that had a branch which reached from Pete and Pam's yard into Jan's yard. He built the tree house and invited all three children to play in it. Jan's dad, Mr. Jones, got quite upset because part of the tree house went over the property line onto his property. He asked Mr. Parsons to either remove the house or fix it so it did not overlap into his yard. Mr. Parsons thought that was silly and refused. Mr. Jones then told Jan not to play with Pete and Pam. All three children were very sad that their dads couldn't seem to work out their dispute and that the problem affected their relationship.*

The Questions:

1. Why do you think Mr. Jones got upset about the tree house?

2. Why do you think Mr. Parsons refused to remove the tree house?

3. What do you think the solution to the problem could have been?

The Feelings:

Pretend that you are the person before you answer the questions below:

1. How do you think Jan felt?

2. How do you think Pam felt?

3. How do you think Pete felt?

4. How do you think Mr. Parsons felt?

5. How do you think Mr. Jones felt?

6. What might each of the people have done to affect the feelings or actions of another?

7. How could all the people involved feel good about this situation?

YOUNG PERSON'S EXERCISE 2

The Candy Game

The purpose of this exercise is to teach (demonstrate) collaborative and cooperative solutions to problems.

The exercise is carried out by two people sitting at a table or lying on the floor. The parent (or other leader) asks that they grasp the hand of the other (presumably the right hand) in arm-wrestling fashion.

Next, the participants are told that each person gets a piece of candy (or gum or a raisin or the like) for each time the arm of the opponent touches the table. The exercise is timed (several minutes are plenty for this to work). They are told to "Start."

The natural instinct is for the parties both to strain to force the opponent's arm down (arm-wrestling style). They will probably try to force the other's arm down and waste valuable running time for the exercise. In fact, soon they should learn that if they *cooperate* by taking turns as to whose arm hits the table voluntarily, they will both get candy (or other reward).

If they should not get the point of the exercise, the parent (or other leader) asks them to repeat the process but this time to see if there is a way for both of them to be rewarded.

Following this exercise the leader should inquire whether the participants can see how cooperation is far more effective than conflict.

YOUNG PERSON'S EXERCISE 3

The Animal Conflict Game

This is another exercise used to give young people a sense of conflict and allow them to begin to identify with what it is like to be in conflict. I often use this process as an ice breaker in opening my training programs. Not only does it allow for identification with conflict, but it is fun (and often funny).

This exercise is designed for a group of four or more participants.

The Game: Ask people to sit in a circle so they can watch the face (and body language) of each other.

Next, tell them you are going to ask them all a question and then ask each one individually.

The Question: If you were an animal in conflict, what animal would you be? Be clear that you are not asking what animal would they like to be—rather, how they actually see themselves in conflict now.

Give the participants a few minutes to think about this question, then ask them to share the animal they see themselves as . . . and *why*.

Be prepared for some interesting answers (and probably a few laughs).

If a participant can't think of an animal right away, ask them a question that might help them, such as: When you are in a conflict situation, are you sly like a fox or timid like a mouse? That should help them come up with an answer. Hearing other people's answers will also help.

This little exercise (ice breaker) can tell a lot about people's styles in conflict. Remember the style considerations of Section One?

YOUNG PERSON'S EXERCISE 4

Thought Provocation About Conflict

The purpose of this exercise is to stimulate participants' thoughts about conflict and ways of dealing with it. This exercise requires paper and a writing instrument. Note that this exercise may be too advanced for younger children. As with most of these exercises, it would work well with an adult group.

Leaders ask the participants to write the following words and (1) write a one-sentence definition and (2) create two sentences or statements using the word:

1. Situation—

2. Problem—

3. Dispute—

4. Conflict—

5. Confrontation—

6. Cooperation—

7. Collaboration—

8. Resolution—

If any participant is having trouble, feel free to help them start thinking about their own definition. A dictionary can help, but the exercise requires the participant's own words (interpretation).

Next, have them share the definitions by either passing them around or reading out loud.

A discussion of the definitions and the sentences is certain to be very lively after participants have done this work.

YOUNG PERSON'S EXERCISE 5

The Seven Simple Steps

This exercise is designed to familiarize participants with the Seven Simple Steps to Ironing Out conflicts and to give them a practical feel for how the steps can work.

Part One (Read the fact statement):

Sam and Doug are classmates. Sam loaned his pocket-knife to Doug when Doug was playing at Sam's house. Doug brought the knife to school one day to show his other friends. This violated school rules and when a teacher saw the knife during a recess, she took it away from Doug. Doug was unhappy about telling Sam, so he didn't say anything for several days. When Sam asked Doug for the knife back, Doug told him it was in the school principal's office. Sam is very angry at Doug and told him he doesn't want to play with him again.

Part Two (List the Seven Simple Steps):

1. Remove all masks.
2. Identify the real problem.
3. Give up a must-win attitude.
4. Develop several possible solutions.
5. Evaluate options and select one.
6. Communicate—in a manner certain to be received.
7. Acknowledge and preserve the value in the relationship.

Part Three:

Participants take the role of either Sam or Doug and apply each of the process steps individually with a view toward reaching a solution to the problem. If there is only one participant, draw two columns on a piece of paper and place the names Sam and Doug at the top of each column. Then proceed to list each thing each person could do for each step of the process. Be certain to do all seven steps for one person before going on to the other.

List or recite the action plan for Ironing Out the conflict between Sam and Doug (which was arrived at using the Seven Steps).

YOUNG PERSON'S EXERCISE 6:

The Dispute Detective

The purpose of this exercise is to be aware of and to observe disputes (conflicts) in oneself and others over a period of time.

Directions: Make a chart (matrix) on a piece of paper. In the left hand column, list the key questions below. Across the top, list dispute numbers (i.e., dispute 1, dispute 2, etc.). Now, keep track of the disputes you participate in, see and/or hear and describe each as to the questions on the left.

	Dispute 1	Dispute 2	Dispute 3
1. *Who* is involved?			
2. *Where* is it happening?			
3. *What* was happening or being said?			
4. *How* did it end?			

20

• •

Resources

I know you have done a gallant and noble job of Ironing Out your own conflicts. That is what this book was designed to enable you to do. But, let's face it, there are going to be those issues which just cannot be handled by you alone. So what do you do? Give up?

No. You find out how and where you can get assistance from the outside and you go for help with the same determination you had when you first tried to handle the situation yourself.

The information provided in this chapter is not exhaustive, but it should give you a good start in your quest for aid in conflict resolution. I have divided this chapter into two parts. The first part deals with resource places and the second part provides some interesting additional reading resources which can further enlighten you with regard to your particular issues.

RESOURCE PLACES

In most areas, the right place to look for assistance with a dispute is a professional mediator. I say this not just because I am one, but because it is a mediator who is trained to assist in resolution of disputes while encouraging a collaborative, non-adversarial approach. Often, mediators are also attorneys or have backgrounds in mental health.

How do you find a mediator?

Start with the phone book. Look first under "Mediation." Some phone books list them under "Arbitration and Mediation." Mediators may be available from either public (non-profit) sources or private practitioners. Be certain to ask the person you call whether or not he/she has experience in the domain of your dispute. If not, ask him or her for a recommendation. Be sure also to ask how much they charge and whether or not they are available for one-on-one consulting (if you should need that). Some mediators will do that. Others will not.

Be aware that mediation is a growing professional field and can include people who have just been trained or have unilaterally proclaimed themselves qualified. At this writing, very few states regulate mediators. Care must be taken to ascertain the background and level of training of anyone you might call for help.

If you cannot find someone in your community, ask an attorney about the names of members of the ADR Committee of the Bar Association, ask someone you know in mental health or ask your clergy person for some guidance.

Some state court systems have offices of dispute resolution. In Virginia, the Office of Dispute Resolution is part of the Office of the Executive Secretary of the State Supreme Court. Check with your local senior court administrator about your area.

If you still cannot locate a mediator, there are several centralized listing places. I have listed below the names and phone numbers of several organizations which can help you find someone. Do not feel shy about calling. If, after trying all other sources, you still cannot find someone suitable, call me at (540) 636-8900.

Society of Professionals in   (202) 783-7277
Dispute Resolution (SPIDR)
(membership organization for
professionals in the field)

The American Bar Association   (202) 331-2258
Standing Committee on Dispute
Resolution (maintains a clearinghouse
of firms, organizations and individuals
and publishes an annual directory)

Conflict Resolution Center International   (412) 481-5559
(maintains clearing house for
international mediators)

Academy of Family Mediators   (800) 292-4236
(professional membership organization
of divorce and family mediators)

National Association of Mediators in   (413) 545-2462
Education (membership group of
mediators involved with education)

Harvard Negotiation Project   (617) 495-1684
(has a comprehensive listing—
public and private)

Martindale-Hubbell   (908) 464-6800
(private firm which publishes directory
of dispute resolution providers)

National Institute of Dispute Resolution   (202) 466-4764
(non-profit consulting, research and
funding organization. Also publishes
resource directory)

International Academy of Commercial   (800) 967-4555
Mediators (membership organization
of non-family mediators)

RESOURCES FOR FURTHER READING

In addition to the books I have cited in the text or in footnotes (which are not repeated below), the list which follows is offered as a cross section of good reading on the subject. This list is not meant to be exhaustive and any author who didn't make it to this list should not feel offended (we can Iron Out our differences):

About Conflicts in General

Coser, *The Functions of Social Conflict* (New York, Free Press, 1964) discusses the positive aspects of conflict.

Crum, *The Magic of Conflict* (Touchstone, Simon & Schuster 1987).

Frank, *Male Sexuality* (New York, Avon, 1969) is an amazingly open and forward looking book (for its time) in which my late uncle, Stanley Frank, discusses the wonderful dynamic between men and women. This groundbreaking book may be hard to find.

Hendrix, *Getting the Love You Want: A Guide for Couples* (New York, Henry Holt, 1985) is about creative use of the "love/hate energy" conflict in marriage.

Jourard, *The Transparent Self* (New York, Van Nostrand Reinhold, 1971) discusses how we can seem to be one thing and do something else. Very relevant to Step One.

Pearce, *Magical Child* (New York, Bantam Books, 1980) comments on the need for stress in child development and expands on Piaget's work.

Pearce, *Magical Child Matures* (New York, E. P. Dutton, 1985) follows on his previous book above and takes the "magical child" into those perplexing years of adolescence and young adulthood. According to Pearce, this is his favorite book.

Piaget, *The Grasp of Consciousness* (Cambridge, Harvard University Press, 1976). Outlines some of the thinking of this major scholar on the importance of stress (conflict) in human development.

About Dispute Resolution Processes

Burton and Dukes, *Conflict Practices in Management, Settlement and Resolution* (New York, St. Martin's Press, 1990) is part of an excellent series by John Burton.

Coulson, *Fighting Fair: Family Mediation Will Work for You* (New York, Free Press, 1983) is one of the earlier family mediation guides.

Folberg and Taylor, *Mediation: A Comprehensive Guide to Resolving Conflict Without Litigation* (San Francisco, Jossey-Bass, 1984) is a good introduction.

Goldberg, Green and Sander, *Dispute Resolution* (Boston, Little Brown, 1985) is one of the most widely accepted introductions to the field.

Janis and Mann, *Decision Making: A Psychological Analysis of Conflict, Choice and Commitment* (New York, Free Press, 1977) discusses more about the relationship of psychology to conflict and what to do about it.

Kagel and Kelly, *The Anatomy of Mediation: What Makes It Work* (Washington, BNA, 1989).

Keltner, *Mediation: Toward a Civilized System of Dispute Resolution* (Annandale, Va., Speech Communication Association, 1987) is one of the best small books on mediation.

Lemmon, *Family Mediation Practice* (New York, Free Press, 1985) is the definitive family mediation process text.

Lickson, *Conflict and Basic Mediation Skills Workbook* (Charlottesville, Va., MLM Publishing Inc., 1991) is a skills workbook and guide to basic skills training.

Lickson, *The Use of Alternative Dispute Resolution in Intellectual Property, Technology-Related or Innovation-Based Disputes* (Rochester, Lawyers Cooperative Publishing, 1995). This article is part of *AmJur's Trials* series. It's a very recent, comprehensive look at the legal bases for alternative dispute resolution.

Lovenheim, *Mediate Don't Litigate* (New York, McGraw-Hill, 1990) is a deservedly popular book in the field.

Moore, *The Mediation Process: Practical Strategies for Resolving Conflict* (San Francisco, Jossey-Bass, 1986) is a book by one of the better-known mediators and trainers in the U.S.

Simkin, *Mediation and the Dynamics of Collective Bargaining* (Washington, Bureau of National Affairs, 1971) is a book by one of the best-known experts in the field.

Singer, *Settling Disputes: Conflict Resolution in Business, Families and the Legal System* (Boulder, Colo., Westview Press, 1990) introduces ADR and looks at directions of development of the field.

About Family Disputes

Crary, Elizabeth, *Kids Can Cooperate: A Practical Guide to Teaching Problem Solving* (Seattle, Parenting Press, Inc., 1984)

Dinkmeyer, Don and Lewis E. Losoncy, *The Encouragement Book* (New York, Fireside/Simon & Schuster, 1992)

Farrell, Warren, *Why Men are the Way They Are: The Male-Female Dynamic* (New York, McGraw Hill, 1986)

Fishel, Ruth, *Five Minutes for World Peace Forever: A 90-Day Affirmation Plan* (Deerfield Beach (Fla.), Health Center, Inc., 1991)

Heldman, Mary L., *When Words Hurt: How to Keep Criticism from Undermining Self Esteem* (New York, New Chapter Press, 1988)

Kaufman, Barry Neil, *Happiness is a Choice* (New York, Faucett Columbini, 1991)

Keirsey, David and Marilyn Bates, *Please Understand Me: The Character and Temperament Types,* Gnosology Books, Ltd. (Del Mar, Prometheus Nemeses Book Company (Distributor), 1984)

Lazarus, Arnold A., *Marital Myths* (San Luis Obispo Impact Publishers, 1985)

McGinnis, Alan Loy, *Bringing Out the Best in People: How to Enjoy Helping Others Excel* (Minneapolis, Augsburg Publishing House, 1985)

Tannen, Deborah, *You Just Don't Understand: Women and Men in Conversation* (New York, Ballentine Books, 1990)

In addition to the books listed above, there are a number of periodical publications which are directly or indirectly involved with dispute resolution issues. I have listed several of these below plus information on how to get the publications:

Alternative Newsletter is published by the Section on Alternative Dispute Resolution of The Association of American Law Schools. Prof. James Boskey is Editor, (201) 642-8811. Contains information geared toward ADR teachers and is an outstanding resource for what's new in print in the field and when and where training is available.

Dispute Resolution Times is published by the American Arbitration Association, 140 West 51st Street, New York, NY 10020, and is dedicated to AAA news (mostly about arbitration, but with some mediation news).

Consensus is a quarterly publication of The Public Disputes Network of the Harvard Program on Negotiation, 513 Pound Hall, Cambridge, MA 02138. Contains much news about events and organizations involved in public disputes. Also, contains listing of major providers of ADR services around the U.S.

Dispute Resolution. Published periodically by the Standing Committee on Dispute Resolution of the American Bar Association, (202) 331-2258. Contains news of the field and occasional articles on ADR topics.

SPIDR News is published by the Society of Professionals in Dispute Resolution, (202) 783-7277. Contains news of people and events regarding the major professional organizations in ADR.

Mediation News is published by the Academy of Family Mediators, (503) 345-1205. The focus is family dispute resolution.

Mediation Quarterly is a scholarly journal sponsored by the Academy of Family Moderators and published by Jossey-Bass Publishers (415) 433-1767.

Mediation Monthly is monthly newsletter on marketing, ethics and other general mediator issues. (815) 399-8407.

Please note that in addition to the publications listed above, many other scholarly and lay publications frequently contain articles and news about conflict and dispute resolution. Your library's *Readers' Guide to Periodical Literature* is a good place to look for additional material on the subject.

References

1. Western Pacific Case. 345 U.S. 247, 270.
2. Warschaw, *Winning By Negotiation* (New York, McGraw-Hill, 1980).
3. Stuart Atkins, Inc., *Discovery Workbook* (Beverly Hills, 1978).
4. Warschaw, pp. 55–63.
5. Hubbard, *Dianetics* (Los Angeles, Bridge Publications, 1986).
6. Dass and Gorman, *How Can I Help?* (New York, Knopf, 1987).
7. Hafen and Fransden, *People Need People* (Evergreen, Colo., Cordillera Press, 1987).
8. Fisher and Urey, *Getting to Yes* (New York, Penguin Books, 1988).
9. Fisher and Urey, p. 77.
10. Coon, *Essentials of Psychology* (St. Paul, West Publishing, 1982), p. 305.
11. Mussen et al., eds., *Concepts in Psychology* (Lexington, Mass., D. C. Heath, 1974).
12. Missildine, *Your Inner Conflicts: How to Solve Them* (New York, Simon & Schuster, 1974).
13. Mahoney, *Self-Change: Strategies for Solving Personal Problems* (New York, W. W. Norton, 1979).
14. Mahoney, pp. 28–29.
15. Gawain, *Creative Visualization* and *Living in the Light* (San Rafael, Calif., Whatever Publishing, 1986).
16. Gawain, *Return to the Garden* (Kauai, Hawaii, New World Library, 1989).
17. Gawain, *Living in the Light,* p. 10.

18. Gould, *Transformations* (New York, Simon & Schuster, 1978).

19. Gilligan, *In A Different Voice* (Cambridge, Mass., Harvard University Press, 1982).

20. Tannen, *You Just Don't Understand* (New York, Ballantine Books, 1990).

21. Bly, *Iron John* (Reading, Mass., Addison-Wesley, 1990).

22. Gaines, *Hell Is My Husband* (Pompano, Fla., Paragraph Publications, 1992). By contrast, read *Don't Go Away Mad* (New York, Doubleday, 1990) by Dr. Jim Creighton—a sensitive book which is aptly subtitled: "How to Make Peace with Your Partner."

23. Balnave, *Computer User's Legal Reporter,* January–February 1990.

24. Conversation between author and Eric Green of JAMS-ENDISPUTE, August 1990.

25. Drucker, *Managing for Results* (New York, Harper & Row, 1964).

26. Covey, *The Seven Habits of Highly Effective People* (New York, Simon & Schuster, 1989).

27. Cohn and Conti, *Employment Relations Today,* Spring 1990.

28. Susskind and Cruikshank, *Breaking the Impasse* (New York, Basic Books, 1987).

29. The Forum, presented in 1988 by Werner Erhard Associates, San Francisco, Calif.

30. Mahoney, p. 15.

31. Waitley, *The Psychology of Winning* (Chicago, Nightingale-Conant, 1986).

32. Mahoney, p. 38. Dr. Mahoney deals with reality. So does the work of William Glasser, M.D., who, along with G. L. Harrington M.D., formulated Reality Therapy. Today it is in use by many professionals in therapy. It provides a solid base for mask removal, being authentic and counseling the *real* issues underlying the problem. An excellent collection of cases based on this theory is contained in *What Are You Doing: How People Are Helped through Reality Therapy,* edited by Naomi Glasser (New York, Harper & Row, 1980).

ABOUT CHARLES P. LICKSON

A former practicing attorney with many years of trial practice, Lickson has been involved in dispute resolution for over thirty years. He received a B.A. in Political Science (with Honors) from Johns Hopkins University and a J.D. from Georgetown Law Center. After serving as a Law Clerk for a federal judge in Washington D.C., and in the U.S. Army during the Vietnam era, Lickson entered the practice of law as a corporate attorney. He entered private practice more than 25 years ago and was a trial and general law practitioner until 1982, when he gave up law practice to enter the business community. Lickson has been a professional, full-time mediator and trainer since 1989. He founded Mediate-Tech, Inc. (MTI), the nation's first technology-ADR firm. He is a frequent speaker and trainer and his articles on ADR, technology and law have appeared in many lay and professional publications. He is the author of *Ethics for Government Employees* and *A Legal Guide for Small Business,* both available from Crisp Publications. Lickson can be reached at MTI (800) 967-4555.